A UNIQUE MEDICINAL PLANT

GALA

HOLY BASIL
TULSI
(A Herb)

by
Yash Rai

NAVNEET PUBLICATIONS (INDIA) LIMITED

Navneet House, Gurukul Road, Memnagar, Ahmadabad – 380 052.
Phone : 745 10 00 / 743 63 00

Navneet Bhavan, B. S. Road, Dadar, Mumbai – 400 028.
Phone : 430 72 86

DHANLAL BROTHERS DISTRIBUTORS
70, Princess Street, Mumbai – 400 002.
Phone : 201 70 27

S 295
G 515

Visit us at : www.navneet.com & connectschool.com

e-mail : npil@navneet.com

Price : Rs. 40.00

Pilgrims Book House Kathmandu

Lovingly dedicated to
Beloved Niece
NAMITA CHAUHAN

© **All rights reserved. No part of this book may be copied, adapted, abridged or translated, stored in any retrieval system, computer system, photographic or other system or transmitted in any form or by any means without the prior written permission of the copyright holders, M/s. Navneet Publications (India) Ltd.** *Any breach will entail legal action and prosecution without further notice.*

TULSI

Yash Rai

1, Matruchhaya Apartments, Opp. Muni. School No. 11, Haripura, Maninagar (East), Ahmadabad–380 008.

Published by   Navneet Publications (India) Ltd., Dantali, Gujarat.
Printed by   Gurukripa Offset, Ahmedabad.

[22–8–2002 (9) : 3]

A UNIQUE MEDICINAL PLANT
TULSI

The Tulsi plant is a shrub of great medicinal value. Its position is unrivalled both in religious sacraments and in therapeutic applications. Its qualities as described in Aryan works expounding Ayurveda are : 'sharp in taste, with a trace of bitterness, easily digestible, hot, dry, destroyer of phlegm (kapha) and gas or wind (vayu or vata), promoting appetite and digestion, fragrant, salubrious, and destroyer of worms and bad odours.' Rearing a Tulsi plant in one's courtyard is considered an essential step towards religious as well as physical well-being.

Its use is beneficial in cases of loss of appetite, colds, crepitation (sasni) and laboured breathing, and highly effective against coughs, pains and nausea. It can be used with advantage in cases of migraine, poisoning, headache, suppuration of the ears, excessive thirst, urticaria, cholera, bad breath (halitosis), worms and pains in the sides and the chest.

Satisfactory results are obtained in the treatment of colds by administering the juices of Tulsi and ginger with honey thrice a day. The sage Charak has also suggested the administration of the juice of the darker variety of Tulsi (Shyama Tulsi) mixed with honey as a remedy for coughs. If there is pus formation in the ears, with consequent emanation of foul odours, drops of Tulsi juice, or of mustard oil boiled with Tulsi juice, may be instilled. In cases of influenza and other cognate fevers, two teaspoonfuls of Tulsi and ginger juices mixed with half a gramme of Tribhuvan Kirti invariably prove beneficial. An attack of asthma can be relieved by two or three doses of a mixture of honey and a brew obtained by boiling five grammes of the inflorescences (manjari) of Tulsi with ten grammes of dry (stone) ginger with a sufficient quantity of water. The brew should be cooled before administering it with honey. Chewing 25 Tulsi leaves a day is advised in case of bad breath. Tulsi in any form should never be taken with milk. Tulsi has anthelmintic and antibiotic properties, and as it augments the capacity of the body to resist and fight diseases, it is potentially useful even against diseases like cancer.

Vatsal Vasani (Ayu Digest : May '78)

Leukaemia can be cured by Tulsi therapy.

– Dr. Upendra Rai J. Sandesara (Ahmadabad)

The case history of Trilokchand Parikh is instructive.

A lump was noticed on the right side of the patient's neck in October 1977. There was also infection in the nasal passages, as well as in the throat. Leukaemia was diagnosed in December 1977. The patient had long-standing diabetes too.

The condition of the patient got progressively worse after that. In 1980 it became serious. Blisters developed due to viral infection of Herpes. Blood was oozing through the skin due to the reduction in the number of platelets. The pain was intolerable. Even the patient's younger brother, who is an M. D. and an M. R. C. P., a renowned consulting physician in Ahmadabad, lost all hope. It was at this juncture that Shri Trilokchand approached me for treatment.

A favourable response to the treatment was noticed in a few days. Gradually, his condition improved. In a blood test carried out on 22-12-'82 his blood was reported to be normal. A year has passed since then. He is now in good health. He walks a few kilometres daily even at his present age of 70–72 years. He is able to carry out his religious rituals and secular functions quite normally.

Similar treatment in other cases of blood cancer and also other types of cancer has effected cures or at least brought the disease under control and afforded relief.

The treatment given is generally along the following lines :

(1) Tulsi is given three or four times a day along with other medication and appropriate 'anupan' – certain nutrients with reinforcing and supplementary action. (2) The patient is given vegetables, germinated green grams (moong), juice of doorva grass, fruits, 'separated' milk (from which fats have been removed), curds, and other foods as prescribed from time to time. (3) The patient is given drinks of 'Tulsi Sudha', which is prepared by boiling Tulsi leaves with cinnamon, cloves, cardamom and jaggery, and mixing the brew with lemon juice

when cold. (4) Salt, sugar and other sweets, tea, coffee, preparations of refined wheat flour, fried foods, tobacco, cigarettes etc. are forbidden. (5) Even if the patient is a non-vegetarian, he is asked to give up meat, fish and eggs. Alcoholic drinks too must be given up, along with other addictions. Actually 'Tulsi Sudha' helps the patient to overcome the craving for alcohol. (6) Such other Nature Cure procedures as are found beneficial and appropriate may also be adopted. (7) Patients are also advised to perform yogic exercises if they are in a condition to do so.

Prayer, and meditation on Deity are of special importance as part of the treatment.

(Shrirangadarshan, January '84)

An Obeisance to Soorya, the Sun God, the Promoter of Bodily Health

आरोग्यं भास्कराद् इच्छेत्
आदित्यः सविता सूर्यःखगःपूषा गभस्तिमान् ।
सुवर्णस्तपनो भानुः स्वर्णिता दिवाकरः ॥

तदेवाग्निस्तदादित्यस्तद्वायुस्तदु चन्द्रमाः ।
तदेव शुक्रं तद् ब्रह्म ता आपःस प्रजापतिः ॥

नमोऽस्तु सूर्याय नमोऽस्तु भानवे ।
नमोऽस्तु वैश्वानर जातवेदसे ॥

ममैतदर्घ्यं प्रतिगृहाण देव ।
देवाधिदेवाय नमो नमस्ते ॥

नमः सवित्रे जगदेकचक्षुषे ।
जगत्प्रसूति-स्थिति-नाशहेतवे ॥

त्रयीमयाय त्रिगुणात्मधारिणे ।
विरंचिनारायण शङ्करात्मने ॥

CONTENTS

- A Goodwill Message 7
- A Philanthropic Act 8
- Tulsi : In My Estimation 10
1. Tulsi : The Elixir of Life 14
2. Tulsi : The Homeopathic Point of View 35
3. Tulsi : The Ayurvedic Point of View 38
4. Tulsi : Tested Therapeutic Applications 47
5. Tulsi : The Beautifier 54
6. Treatment of Snake-bite, Stings of Insects and other Poisons 56
7. Tulsi : A Remedy for All Fevers 60
8. Diseases of Women 69
9. Diseases of Men 72
10. Diseases of Children 77
11. Vata Disorders, Rheumatism and Painful Joints .. 82
12. Colds, Coughs and other Respiratory Diseases 85
13. Blisters, Boils, Wounds and Skin Diseases 92
14. Diseases of the Digestive System 98
15. Diseases of the Mouth, Teeth, Eyes, Ears, Nose and Throat 107
16. Diseases of the Heart, Flanks, Head and other Miscellaneous Diseases 111
17. Tulsi : Preparation of Medicinal Formulations 116
18. Tulsi : Readymade Formulations 125

A GOODWILL MESSAGE

Timings : 9.00 – 11.30 A.M.
4.00 – 7.00 P.M.

Phone : 386 72 75
SUNDAY CLOSED

EYE-CARE AND VISUAL TRAINING CENTRE

* Dr. D. R. Gala
* Dr. Dhiren Gala
* Dr. Sanjay Gala

Drishti Sudhar Kendra
Abbas Building, 1 'A', 1st Floor,
Opp. Tilak Market,
Jalbhai Road,
Grant Road (East),
Mumbai – 400 004.

Date : 13–6–'88

Dear Shri Yash Rai,

I am returning herewith the manuscript on 'Tulsi', compiled by you. I have studied it thoroughly from beginning to end. I feel that it is likely to prove extremely useful, and will receive eulogies from all readers.

One can hardly realize that there is so much information to be given about tulsi. Please accept my heartiest congratulations.

I would suggest that you continue your researches in this and allied areas.

We intend to try out some of the remedial procedures recommended in the book in our proposed 'Nature Cure' Hospital at Valsad in Gujarat on an experimental basis.

The extensive nature of your reading is obvious from the numerous quotations from the books and periodicals which have been included in the book.

On the whole the book is well-compiled. It testifies to the vast amount of labour that has gone into its making. Perhaps adoption of the pseudonym 'Tulsi Das' would not be inappropriate !

Your sincere well-wisher
(Dr.) D. R. Gala

A PHILANTHROPIC ACT

Tulsi is a plant quite familiar to all. This plant, which grows in all places and under a wide variety of conditions, holds a position of sanctity and importance in our religion and generally in Indian culture as well. Nearly all of our scriptures have sung its praises.

The very name Tulsi, that which cannot be compared, the 'Incomparable One', indicates its great value. Various sagas of Tulsi are found in numerous legends, tales relating to religious observances and rituals, as well as in many anecdotes narrated in the Puranas, our religious scriptures. It is depicted as Vrindā, the wife of Jalandhara in the Padma Purana. Its origin is narrated in the Brahmakhanda, one of the four parts of Brahmavaivarta Purana. The incomparably beauteous Tulsi, the daughter of King Dharmadhwaja, was the incarnation of a Gopi, who had been laid under a curse by Radha because she had dared to aspire to favours from Lord Krishna in Golok. Tulsi is accorded the sixth place among the eight objects of worship in the ritual of the consecration of the Kalasha, the container of holy water. In fact, Tulsi is indispensable in any religious ritual or act of worship.

Tulsi used to be worshipped in the rituals of the Greek (Eastern) Church, and every year on the Birth Anniversary of Saint Basil, women used to sanctify their houses by scattering Tulsi leaves which had been previously offered in churches, inviting the saint's blessings to bestow good fortune on the family in the new year.

But apart from the religious significance, Tulsi is of great importance in another field : medicine. Charak, Dhanvantari, Sushrut and other great physicians and pharmacologists have unanimously accorded it an eminent position as a therapeutic agent. Along with a large number of references to Puranas and other prestigious Sanskrit works, this book [Tulsi] describes numerous applications of Tulsi in the Ayurvedic system of medicine, and enumerates its medicinal qualities.

Tulsi is 'Surasā', containing beneficent fluids. Tulsi juice in moderate amounts enhances the physical beauty of a person. Tulsi is the most effective destroyer of kapha (phlegm) and pitta (bile), benefits the heart, removes toxins, increases the secretion and quality of semen, and strengthens memory. Diarrhoea, piles, kidney stones, anorexia (loss of appetite), skin diseases, worms, acne, eczema, body odours, foetal diseases, infertility, sterility, labour pains, constipation, colic, toothache, earache, dysuria, urethritis, vomiting, asthma, hiccups, fevers, diseases of the mouth, ailments of the eyes, anaemia, leprosy, excessive thirst, gonorrhoea, abnormalities of *vayu* (wind) leading to neuritis, colour blindness, tetanus, fainting, allergy are among the many conditions that can be successfully treated with Tulsi. The presentation of a plethora of remedial applications of Tulsi in a form understandable to laymen is really a philanthropic act on the part of the author.

('Gujarat Mitra' : 18-4-'88) Jayant Chauhan

TULSI : IN MY ESTIMATION

For thousands of years, Indian culture has accorded a position of great importance to trees, herbs and other components of the natural environment. Our Vedic literature too has recognized the importance of plants for the wealth, prosperity and health of human life. Ayurveda, considered to be an additional Veda and indeed ranked on an equal footing with the four ancient Vedas, has also recognised the therapeutic qualities of trees, shrubs and herbs, and their valuable contributions to the maintenance of physical and mental health. This is the reason why even in our daily lives we have come to look upon trees and herbs with a kind of respect and religious faith.

In our rural areas, trees and plants had become an integral part of social life. Most of our religious festivals included worship of trees. Trees acquired importance from not only the religious point of view, but also that of art and decoration. Neem, peepul, banyan, asopalav and other trees became indispensable in our lives. Among all these trees, shrubs and herbs, Tulsi occupies the most respected and sanctified position, a position of importance whether considered from the point of view of health, or religion, or metaphysics, or even decorative value.

The Tulsi plant in the courtyard of every Hindu house is a unique symbol of the aesthetic sense, the culture, the sanctity and religious inclinations of the family. Some well-to-do families have the Tulsi planted in a specially built structure. The images of the deity in whom the family has the greatest faith are installed on all four sides of the structure. Pure soil fertilised with cow-dung is spread at the centre of the top of the structure and a Tulsi plant reared with devotional care. In some households, eight or ten Tulsi plants are reared in the verandah or adjoining ground, forming a 'Tulsi-van' or 'Vrindavan', a miniature forest of sanctifying plant.

Every Hindu housewife, in her daily routine, after her morning ablutions, carries out pooja or dedicatory worship. Then she goes and pours the holy water from the pooja into the soil supporting the Tulsi plant, spreads the pallav of her saree in obeisance, and prays for the bestowal of prosperity, peace of mind and happiness on the family. The Tulsi plant is again worshipped in the evening, and a deepak, a small lamp burning pure ghee, is lighted before it. During the four months of the monsoon, designated 'Chaturmas' in the Hindu almanac, the daily worship of Tulsi becomes an important and indispensable religious ritual. Thus the location of the Tulsi plant in front of the residence of every respectable Hindu householder has for ages held sway as a symbol of Hindu culture augmenting the spiritual beauty and promoting the material prosperity and well-being of the household. The Hindu scriptures enjoin us to look upon Tulsi not as a mere plant, but as the divine representative of the God Vishnu or of Lord Krishna. Ayurveda has depicted in great detail the importance of the medicinal qualities of Tulsi. The contribution of the Tulsi plant to the purification of polluted air is unrivalled which is perhaps the reason why Tulsi plants have been growing in lush profusion in Lord Krishna's 'Vrindavan' ! No act of worship, no pooja ritual of God Vishnu or Lord Krishna is considered complete without the presence of 'Tulsipatra', the leaves of the Tulsi plant. Nor is any 'prasad', the offerings to a deity which are sanctified and returned to the worshipper as the symbol of the benediction of the deity, acceptable as 'prasad' unless the offering includes the Tulsi leaves.

The detailed description of the qualities and special characteristics of Tulsi given in this book will enable the reader to appreciate its importance. The Tulsi plant is so familiar and so easily obtainable everywhere that people tend to take it for granted. There is a saying in Sanskrit that even a thing of great importance or a person of great endowments appears common and ordinary to persons familiar with them. The English saying is harsher, and asserts that 'Familiarity breeds contempt'. Tulsi has not become an object of contempt, but its importance has certainly come to be disregarded because of its familiarity.

We have forgotten its invaluable qualities, and by taking costly foreign allopathic medicines for disorders that can be cured easily and without any expenditure by utilizing the curative properties of the Tulsi plant, we incur financial losses and harm ourselves.

Tulsi has conferred so many benefits on us, that we are under obligation to treat it with perfect faith and respect while taking advantage of its special qualities.

The Tulsi plant can be used for : (1) prevention as well as (2) cure of illnesses. A Tulsi plant at the doorstep of a house keeps the atmosphere pure, keeps mosquitoes away, supplies oxygen when we need greater supplies of oxygen due to increased rates of respiration while taking exercise, and even study is benefited if carried on in the proximity of a Tulsi plant.

That the Almighty has created the Tulsi plant with its unrivalled qualities for our well-being is surely an indication of His infinite benevolence towards us !

If we rear a Tulsi plant in front of our houses, or at the back of the houses, in galleries, windows or other places where it is exposed regularly to sunlight, we are sure to be granted long and healthy life and everlasting beauty. There would be no need to have recourse to external aids and therapies to attain beauty and health.

I am extremely grateful to the respected scholar Dr. D. R. Gala and to my friend Dr. Dhiren Gala for taking a deep interest in the preparation of the book and for their valuable advice and guidance. I feel honoured by the fact that a prestigious firm like Gala Publishers is publishing this book.

It is my ardent desire and hope that everyone will attain perfect health and enjoy a long life by the conscientious and faithful use of Tulsi in the daily life and affairs.

— **Yash Rai**

> "Companion of Lakshmi,
>
> Benevolence personified,
>
> Liberator from sins and awarder of religious merit,
>
> Dear to Lord Narayan, whose praises are incessantly sung by the sage Naradji,
>
> O Mother Tulsi ! I bow down in worship to thee."
>
> There is nothing greater than a Brahmin, Tulsi, Peepul tree, Cow and the river Ganga.
>
> Always seek association with these five.
>
> No disease visits the house that has a cow and a Tulsi plant its courtyard.
>
> This is the essence of all rules of health.
>
> "A house with a Tulsi plant in front of it is a place of pilgrimage. The messengers of Yama, the God of Death, cannot enter such a house. The wind that carries the aroma of Tulsi spreads purity wherever it blows."

1. TULSI : THE ELIXIR OF LIFE

At the break of dawn, purified and sanctified by her morning ablutions, bearing the auspicious tokens of her blessed conjugal state, her heart full of the sacred sweetness of the morning and the sentiment of love, as the mistress of a household extends her hand to place the lamp with the wick of devotion fed by the oil of faith before the Tulsi plant...... have you seen the radiance that illuminates her face ? With the limitless devotion for Tulsi lighting up her face with divine light, and the hope of endless conjugal bliss lighting up her heart, her face appears no less tender, no less holy than God's companion Tulsi herself. In an instant her heart fills with beatitude as she bows down to Tulsi. She takes up her daily household duties with renewed vigour and enthusiasm.

As evening dusk approaches, the same lady, forgetting the fatigue of her day's chores, having purified herself by another bath, returns with the zeal and pleasurable anticipation of a daughter returning to her mother, to light a lamp before the Tulsi plant and offer her obeisances.

"No disease visits the house that has a cow and Tulsi at its doorstep." We would be well advised to sit in the lap of Tulsi, whose greatness is embodied in the above dictum, and try to cultivate more intimate acquaintance with this representative of God.

Tulsi is itself worshipped, and its leaves offered to God in worship. Its leaves are accorded primacy in religious rituals, in the 'prasad' offered to Gods, as also in devotional worship, in the preparation of the salubrious mixture known as 'Panchamrit' and in alms to the poor. In Greece, too, people have a great faith in Tulsi worship. The Greeks celebrate a 'Tulsi day' every year in honour of Tulsi. Tulsi is used as a household remedy in Australia too. Tulsi possesses hundreds of medicinal virtues. This is the reason why the sages of Ayurved exercised foresight and accorded such importance to Tulsi, establishing the tradition of growing Tulsi plants in all homes, declaring that fear, disease and unhappiness can never gain entry into a home with a Tulsi plant in front of it. It is even believed that the messengers of the God of Death (i.e., diseases) cannot approach a home where there is a Tulsi plant!

In the Vedas it has been ordained that God does not accept any offering if it does not include Tulsi leaves.

In the Puranas Tulsi has been described as the consort of Lord Krishna. Thus Tulsi has been given the apellation of 'Mother of the Universe'. Another name given to Tulsi is 'Vrindā'. That has led to the hallowed region where Lord Krishna indulged in His childhood pranks to be known as 'Vrindāvan'.

The infinite reverence exhibited towards Tulsi in the Hindu religion is not entirely due to unreasoning religious beliefs, but rests upon solid scientific foundations. In addition to its spiritually uplifting qualities, Tulsi has been found to possess extraordinary powers of healing and promoting health. This fact has been confirmed by the researches of modern chemists, who state that Tulsi possesses a special capacity of killing harmful micro-organisms. Thus the wind that carries the fragrance of Tulsi spreads health and well-being wherever it blows.

From the point of view of therapeutic effect, Tulsi is not merely a healing agent, not merely a medicine, but it is a medicine par excellence, the veritable elixir of life, because all the diseases that afflict mankind can be cured by Tulsi. Tulsi is not merely worshipped by people who rear it in their courtyards; they utilise its medicinal virtues too. They are, therefore, never ill. A person that eats even five leaves of Tulsi a day is protected from a large number of diseases. Common illnesses are kept away, or get cured without any further treatment or medication. There is no need of going to a physician for coughs, colds, fevers, toothache, stomachache, headache, sore throat, nasal discomfort, eye diseases, inflammation, itching, loss of appetite, indigestion, vomiting, diarrhoea, dysentery, heart disease, worms, rheumatism, boils, cuts, wounds, skin diseases, acne, irritation, pustules caused by plucking of hair, sunstroke, muscular pains, nocturnal emissions, fainting, poisoning, etc., and most common diseases of women and children. One can treat oneself successfully with a fair knowledge of Tulsi therapy. Other more severe illnesses can also be controlled with the help of experienced *Vaidyas*, physicians well versed in Ayurvedic therapeutics. In view of all this it is not at all inappropriate to term Tulsi 'The Elixir of Life'.

We cannot reap the full advantages of Tulsi unless it is grown on a large scale. Tulsi plants must be raised in every home. Citizens must be given training in Tulsi therapy for the cure of common ailments. Every village must have its 'Vrindāvan', so that Tulsi leaves are always easily available in sufficient quantities for preparing medicinal formulations. Organizations or firms manufacturing Ayurvedic medicines should serve the people by including Tulsi-based medicines in their products, as part of their obligation to society.

For ensuring the purity of air in our homes, we should plant a few Tulsi plants in pots and place the pots during the day in every one of the rooms we commonly use. The pots may be taken out into the open in the evenings and left there overnight, to be brought back in the morning. This will keep the atmosphere in the house fresh, and a number of disorders and atmospheric pollution will be prevented.

If we propagate the use of Tulsi, we shall be conferring a very great benefit on the common people. Some of the important considerations in this connection are the following:

(1) Tulsi should be grown extensively so that it is available in sufficient quantities for medicinal preparations.

(2) Health centres dispensing only medicines prepared from Tulsi should be established. Just as the standard Ayurvedic preparations like Chyavanprash, Drakshasav, etc. are freely available in the market, Tulsi tablets, Tulsi syrups,

TULSI : THE ELIXIR OF LIFE

Tulsi powders, Tulsi extract, etc., should be made by modern standardized processes and sold in the market.

(3) Tea is a stimulant, but it contains a harmful substance called tannin. But Tulsi contains no such harmful substance. Only Tulsi tea should therefore be taken in the morning, afternoon and evening.

(4) A project for rearing a Tulsi-van or for establishing a Tulsi Sanatorium would also be beneficial in every way. It would also be practically very easy to provide for. In any village, even fifty or a hundred square yards of land would be sufficient for such a project. The local people will reap the numerous benefits of a Tulsi garden at nominal expense. **And if some of the therapeutic procedures of the Nature cure system can also be made available in the Tulsi-van, success exceeding such as falls to the lot of even eminent physicians and surgeons can easily be obtained in rooting out pernicious and even fatal diseases.**

(5) Tulsi has the power of purifying the atmosphere. If some organization arranges to supply Tulsi saplings in pots at no, or nominal, cost, it will be making a valuable contribution to the spread of this natural agency for de-polluting the atmosphere. Owners of bungalows and tenements can also contribute to the public weal by raising a few Tulsi plants along with the other flower plants in their grounds. It will help in checking the proliferation of mosquitoes, flies, and other harmful insects, and render the atmosphere healthy. Even people having no open ground can easily raise one or two Tulsi plants in their homes.

Man has been hearing two words from the dawn of civilization : disease and medicine. Any physical discomfort makes us think at once of medicines, such as tablets, injections, mixtures, capsules, etc. But in the past these modern forms of medicines were unknown. The only medicines known and used were some herbs. And these were sufficient to effect speedy cures of even the most terrible diseases. Tulsi was one such medicinal plant known to the ancients.

When the sages of old came to know through experimentation that this plant is capable of curing not one, not two, but hundreds of serious disorders, and that in addition, it keeps the surrounding atmosphere pure and healthy, they made various efforts to ensure wide cultivation of this plant. They included the rearing of at least one Tulsi plant in every home, and caring for it, as a part of a religious duties. They also insisted on growing large numbers of Tulsi plants in Tulsi-vans at important religious places, so that their salutary effects would purify the atmosphere over a wide area.

Gradually, as the salubrious and salutary properties of Tulsi became known, people came to revere it as a holy plant. This resulted in a great increase in the usefulness of Tulsi, because when something is used with trust and faith, its effects become stronger and more rapid. As is well-known, the ancient Ayurvedic works recommend that whenever the medicinal herbs are collected for storage or use, they should be eulogised and prayed to, before they are plucked. The plucking or cutting has also to be done at certain auspicious times connected with the positions of the constellations and the phases of the moon, the purpose being to ensure that they are picked with care and reverence, rather than carelessly and wantonly. Such a positive attitude is bound to increase their efficacy.

Tulsi has a salutary effect not only on the body, but also on the thoughts, tendencies and inclinations of the mind. Our scriptures enjoin us to estimate the worth of a substance not only from its easily observable characteristics, but also to take into consideration all its effects *in toto,* the gross as well as the subtle ones. Tulsi helps not only in curing physical ailments such as fevers, coughs, colds, etc., but also in promoting purity, sanctity and faith.

These eulogies of Tulsi are not simply prompted by flights of fancy. The Indians have been experiencing the benefits conferred by Tulsi for thousands of years. It is for this reason that Tulsi has found a place in every temple, every place of pilgrimage and in every respectable home. Even today numerous people with a modern outlook, in India and outside India, recognize its qualities and arrange to have pots of the Tulsi plants in their houses to keep the air pure and fresh. And a Tulsi plant is sure to act as a centre for spreading positive and ennobling thoughts.

Thus whatever our motives may be in keeping up a close association with Tulsi, we are sure to benefit physically, mentally and spiritually by the association. It was because of this recognition of the benefits Tulsi can bring, that the sages who wrote our scriptures authored tales extolling the greatness of Tulsi, to ensure its popularity among the common people. The result was the almost universal tradition of rearing the Tulsi plants.

The ancient poets have thus eulogised Tulsi and described the numerous benefits conferred by it to secure a place for it in the affections of the people. Out of these the therapeutic benefits relating to the body can be easily experienced at first hand. All works dealing with the science of health according to the Ayurveda describe the efficacy of Tulsi in curing a large number of diseases, especially coughs, colds, fevers, etc., among the remedies for which Tulsi enjoys a prominent position.

Tulsi has been described as sharp in taste, but this quality is limited to a peculiar odour and its capacity to kill germs. Tulsi is a domestic plant with no harmful effects, and as such it is the best of all the medicinal herbs. Tulsi is taken generally with 'prasad' offerings, with water rendered hold by washing the feet of Gods, and with the salubrious mixture of five ingredients, the 'panchamrita'. Thus in a sense it is a part of our diet. As Tulsi is always used when it is fresh, and in its natural state, there is no possibility of its generating toxins in the body. A large number of household remedies for common daily use can be prepared by mixing Tulsi with dry (stone) ginger, pepper, billa fruit pulp, the tender shoots of the neem tree, cardamom, and such other curative ingredients.

Thus the use of Tulsi as a medicine has no adverse side effects, nor does it result in the accumulation of toxins in the body. Tulsi improves the efficiency of all the organs of the body in a natural way and thus helps in the cure of diseases. Unlike the various types of toxic and corrosive substances contained in the injections given for quick results by allopathic doctors and the different types of bhasmas (produced by calcination of various substances) used by *Vaidyas* (Ayurvedic doctors), there is no reason to fear any reactions or deleterious effects when Tulsi is used as a therapeutic agent. This is a plant of such a benign nature that no harmful effect has been observed even on persons who have consumed ten or twenty of its leaves at a time.

Laymen know of only two varieties of Tulsi : Ram Tulsi and Shyam Tulsi. The leaves of Ram Tulsi are rather lighter in colour, which has earned it the apellation of 'Gori', the fair one. Shyam, or 'Krishna' Tulsi, is rather darker in colour and is more effective as a destroyer of *kapha* (phlegm). Consequently it is 'Krishna' Tulsi that is generally preferred for medicinal uses, as its aroma and its juice possess the property of being 'sharp' to a greater extent. There are numerous therapeutic procedures given in this book under the heading 'Tulsi Therapy'. Unless otherwise specified, Tulsi in that context should always be understood to be Krishna Tulsi.

There is another variety of Tulsi, called 'Vana Tulsi', also known as 'kutherak'. It has a much stronger aroma than the domestic variety, and its capacity to neutralise poisons is correspondingly greater. This variety is particularly useful in the treatment of toxaemia, leucoderma, eye diseases and obstetric diseases. There is a fourth variety of Tulsi, called 'maruvak'. According to an opinion expressed in the prestigious work 'Ramamārtanda', the juice of this variety of Tulsi is beneficial when applied to cuts, wounds or bruises, as also to bites of poisonous animals. A fifth variety is 'Barbari' or 'Babui', the tender shoots of which have a penetrating odour. In the Hakeemi or Unani system, the seeds of this Tulsi are referred to as 'Tukhm Rehan'. This variety has the property described as Vajikaran, making a man as strong as a horse. It is used to make semen thicker.

Other varieties of Tulsi are found in various regions. All of them share the qualities of possessing strong odour and antibiotic and anthelmintic properties.

Malaria is endemic to many parts of India. The disease spreads through mosquito bites, particularly in the latter half of the rainy season. Now the Tulsi plants repel mosquitoes, and chewing a few of its leaves destroys the poisons that are responsible for malaria. This is why a drink of a decoction of Tulsi and pepper is believed to be the surest and the easiest remedy for fevers. Allopathic doctors use quinine for this purpose. But quinine is so drastic in its action that though the temperature is brought down, many other harmful side effects such as headaches, singing in the ears, etc., are caused by internal conversion of heat. These make it necessary to take antidotes like milk, orange juice, etc., which however are too expensive for the common man. The use of Tulsi is comparatively quite cheap, and can cure most types of fevers. In this book, details of the modes of using Tulsi and Tulsi-based medicines are given in later chapters.

Now let us consider the importance of Tulsi from the Ayurvedic point of view. Tulsi is one of the most useful plants of India. It grows wild, and can also be cultivated. The plant is 3 to 4 feet tall. It grows in all types of soils, but black sticky and moist soil is particularly suitable for it. The plants do not need much care or attention. If black soil from a field is taken in a flower pot, Tulsi seeds planted in it and watered regularly, the seeds germinate in a few days. The plant bears inflorescences about 2 inches long. The maximum diameter of the trunk may be about that of a wrist, and the branch stems may grow to the thickness of about half an inch, i.e., about the width of fingers. The leaves are of an elongated oval shape with serrations. There are two main varieties of Tulsi : (1) Shyam Tulsi (with dark stems and leaves), and

(2) Ram Tulsi (with whitish stems and light green leaves). Both the varieties are almost equally efficacious in medicinal applications, and the aroma also does not differ much. Still, however, the darker Shyam Tulsi is a little 'hotter' and stronger in its effects.

It is necessary for us to develop an understanding of the properties of Tulsi both collectively and analytically. Tulsi is sharp, bitter, hot; it benefits the heart, stimulates appetite, causes a burning sensation and increases the secretion of bile. It cures leucoderma, dysuria, toxaemia and pain in the flanks, and neutralizes phlegm and gas (*kapha* and *vayu*). Normally only the leaves of the plant are used medicinally. Occasionally, however, the seeds are also used.

The juice of Tulsi is sharp, bitter, and has the properties of stimulating hunger and the formation of semen. It has curative effects in cases of pain in the flanks (side stitches), inflammation, worms, hiccups, vomiting, coughs, laboured breathing, fevers, etc. Some British doctors go so far as to designate Tulsi as the prime remedy for some of the diseases generally regarded as incurable. Tulsi is venerable, sacred and a promoter of health.

The practitioners of the Unani system regard Tulsi as hot in the initial stages and dry in the later stages, and believe that it stimulates the activity of the brain, reduces swellings, destroys gas, relieves congestion in the heart, stimulates the appetite, counters dilapidation of the skin and vitiation of the blood. The presence of a Tulsi plant in a house destroys insects, especially bedbugs and lice. It purifies the air. Ram Tulsi is hot and dry in action. It cleanses the nostrils, strengthens the heart, the liver and the stomach, helps digestion, reduces inflammation, has beneficial effects in all disorders related to mental distress, though it may cause headaches and is generally insalubrious for persons with physiological natures classified as 'hot' in Ayurvedic terms. It is beneficial in swellings caused by excessive mucal congestion caused by kapha, as well as in disorders caused by cold surroundings, and it destroys worms lodging in the alimentary canal.

Unani physicians use the name 'Rehan' for Tulsi and its seeds are called 'Tukhm Rehan'. The seeds are believed to be hot in the initial stages, and dry in later stages. They are highly beneficial in cases of dysentery, diarrhoea, dry cough and pulmonary congestion leading to wheezing sounds while breathing. They also induce the production of more concentrated semen. If must be noted that the seeds are not widely used in our country.

Allopathy regards Tulsi as an expectorant, and as a cure for malaria and many other diseases. Tulsi is especially useful in cold-induced disorders such as coughs, backache, bronchitis, pneumonia, influenza and cholera. Tulsi seeds are also used as diuretics, and for facilitating urination.

The Tulsi plants grow wild in all warm regions in general, and are also cultivated in orchards and gardens. Tulsi does not grow well in cold regions.

Some physicians well-versed in Ayurveda believe Shyam Tulsi to possess greater medicinal value. But both the main varieties of Tulsi are actually very similar in this respect. The darker and lighter coloured varieties of Tulsi are well-known in certain regions as 'Shyama' and 'Rama' respectively. Out of the many varieties of Tulsi, five are of special importance in different regions : (1) Krishna Tulsi, (2) Drudriha Tulsi, (3) Ram Tulsi, (4) Babi Tulsi and (5) Tukashmiya.

(1) Krishna Tulsi : This variety is found in almost all regions of India. It is used in the treatment of infection of the throat and the respiratory system, cough, enteric fever, nasal lesions, infected wounds, earache, urinary disorders, skin diseases, etc.

(2) Drudriha Tulsi : This variety is found mainly in Bengal, Nepal, Chatgaon and Maharashtra. Its use purifies the gaseous humour in the body known in Ayurvedic terminology as Apaan Vayu. It relieves dryness of the throat, lubricates the throat and reduces the viscosity of phlegm. It cures inflammation of hands and feet, and rheumatism.

(3) Ram Tulsi : This variety of Tulsi is found in China, Brazil, Eastern Nepal, as well as in Bengal, Bihar, Chatgaon and the southern states of India. The plant is a highly branched shrub, growing to a height of 4 to 8 feet. All the parts of the plant emit a strong aroma. The leaves are 2 to 4 inches in length, pointed and with serrated edges. The plant bears inflorescences of a pale yellow colour. The ovaries are of a flattened spheroidal shape. Ram Tulsi has a characteristic fragrance. Crushing its leaves between the palms releases a stronger fragrance than do other varieties of Tulsi.

This variety of Tulsi is used to treat major diseases like leprosy. The plants are of two types, male and female. Treatment with only the appropriate type of the plant will yield the expected benefit, depending on whether it is a male or a female who is to be treated, and whether it is the left or the right side that is to be treated. Disorders of female and of the left side of the body can be more successfully treated using the female type of Ram Tulsi, and disorders of male, and of the right side of the body yield more easily for treatment with the male type of Ram Tulsi.

(4) Babi Tulsi : This variety of Tulsi is found mainly in the hot and the temperate regions of India, particularly from Punjab to Travancore. It is also found in Bengal, Bihar, Oudh (Avadh), Persia, etc. The plant grows to a height of 1 to 2 feet. The stem and the branches are green or light yellow. The leaves are about 1 to 2 inches long, oval, pointed and sharp. The ends of branches are laden with inflorescences. The ovaries are located in the inflorescences. The seeds are small in size, black in colour, slightly elongated, round at one end and flattened at the other, with thick edges. They possess no fragrance, but they have an oily and sharp, tingling taste. They become sticky when soaked in water. The plant exudes a pleasing aroma when dried. If an extract of all the parts of the plant (roots, twigs, leaves, etc.) is prepared, oil is found floating on the surface of the extract. This oil is yellowish in colour, and slightly volatile, and thickens and solidifies if stored for a few days.

This kind of Tulsi is hot, dry, sharp and bitter. It stimulates nerve-endings, thus causing a tingling sensation. It induces appetite, promotes digestion, benefits the heart, increases the secretion of bile, and is easy to digest. It reduces phlegm and gas, purifies the blood, reduces the burning sensation in the stomach caused by acidity, helps in the elimination of poisons, and has a curative action in cases of eye diseases, worms, itching, vomiting, earache, leucoderma and fevers. It facilitates delivery and cures all disorders incidental to confinement.

Its leaves taste like cloves, and so are widely used for flavouring vegetables etc.

Its seeds have a soothing and cooling action. They possess stimulating, diuretic, and diaphoretic qualities, and are highly nutritious. They reduce inflammation and swelling. The seeds are usually eaten after soaking them in water, sometimes with chapaties.

(5) Tukashmiya : This variety of Tulsi is found in western regions of India and in Persia. It finds use in the treatment of throat disorders, acidity and leprosy. It imparts strength to weakened muscles.

Common Uses of Tulsi : Usually malaria, cholera and many diseases that owe their existence to a weakened state of the body tend to spread more easily during transition periods between the seasons, when atmospheric conditions are changing. The threat of such diseases can be eliminated by circumambulations around a Tulsi plant daily in the morning and evening. The atmosphere is purified, and pure water and air are rendered even purer by the fragrance of the Tulsi plant.

'Tulsi' is a Sanskrit appellation. 'Tulam' is 'similarity', and the word Tulsi means one that does not tolerate, does not permit parity or similarity, one that is incomparable. Because of the salubrity of its juice it is also termed 'Surasā'. Because of its easy availability it is also called 'Sulabhā', the easily obtainable one. As it generally grows more abundantly in rural areas, it has been named 'Grāmyā', the village maiden. It has also earned the name 'Shoolaghni', because of its ability to alleviate pain.

The Latin name given to Tulsi in botanical terminology is 'Ocimum Sanctum'. Charak has described it as a destroyer of coughs, hiccups, poisons and pain in the flanks. It promotes secretion of bile and neutralises *kapha* and *vayu*. As it dispels the unpleasant odours of decaying matter, Charak has termed it 'Pootigandhahā'. According to Sushrut it cures asthma. Dhanvantari, the author of 'Nighantu', has described Tulsi as easily digestible, hot, dry, a destroyer of phlegm, a killer of worms, an apperitif and a stimulator of digestion.

According to Pandit Bhavamishra, the author of 'Bhavaprakash', Tulsi is beneficial for the heart, and cures skin diseases, dysuria and toxaemia.

One of the English names for Tulsi is 'the Mosquito Plant'. Long ago in the British period, Sir George Birdward wrote an article in the *Times* about this plant. In that article it is stated that the Victoria Gardens and the Prince Albert Museum were 'malarial', as they were infested with mosquitoes. Cultivation of the Tulsi plants freed these areas from mosquitoes, and now they are no longer malarial places.

Dr. Narendra Singh, the Assistant Director of the Pharmacology Department of King George Medical College, Lucknow, has carried out extensive investigations on Tulsi. In his opinion, Tulsi possesses 'powerful medicinal properties'. Tulsi is beneficial in heart disease, peptic ulcer, high blood pressure, colitis and asthma. Another property of Tulsi is its 'anti-stress' action. Daily drinks of Tulsi decoction or chewing a few Tulsi leaves regularly every day will relieve the mental stresses generated in our day-to-day struggle for existence, and increase the probability of a long and healthy life. In one of the experiments carried out by the research group led by Dr. Singh to ascertain the degree of protection and curative action of Tulsi against the deleterious effects of physical, chemical and biological stresses, they fed some mice on a diet which included Tulsi in an adequate proportion, and then injected each of them with carbon tetrachloride. It had been established earlier that such an injection has a destructive action on the liver which proves fatal. But the mice that had been fed Tulsi survived !

A special kind of vapour is released by a Tulsi plant into the atmosphere, which purifies the atmosphere. This is actually an essential oil present in the Tulsi plant, which evaporates and spreads through the air, rendering it free from bacteria and other substances likely to cause diseases. A Tulsi plant reared at the doorstep of a house, or in its vicinity, ensures the health of its occupants, and keeps it free from poisonous insects. Tulsi is particularly effective in combating malaria, and has proved to be the best and easiest means of keeping at bay the insects responsible for the spread of malaria, viz. mosquitoes. The emanations from a Tulsi plant are in fact fatal to mosquitoes. Even snakes cannot tolerate the aroma of Tulsi, and keep away from it.

The Tulsi plants should be reared in pots and kept in the home to keep the air fresh and pure. Though it is a very common plant, it is an infallible remedy for many major and minor illnesses that are otherwise difficult to cure. It is these qualities of Tulsi that have made it worthy of worship.

In case of severe cold spasms preceding fevers, Sushrut has suggested rubbing the body of the patient with Tulsi leaves. A malaria patient is benefited if given two teaspoonfuls of pure Tulsi juice every morning and evening. This should preferably be accompanied by administration of one gramme of Tribhuvan Kirti Rasa with enough honey to make a paste. Quinine-based drugs may also be given as advised by the doctor. A person subject to recurrent attacks of malaria would be well advised to chew five to seven well-washed leaves of Tulsi every morning and evening. Tulsi should be regularly taken in the monsoon and the former half of the winter season. The usual manner of taking Tulsi is to chew its leaves. The Atharvaveda considers Tulsi to be a purifier of blood. Tulsi is effective in the treatment of pneumonia too. Ayurveda regards Tulsi as an expectorant, an efficient diuretic, a promoter of digestion and a purifier of blood. Tulsi is an infallible remedy for colds. Tulsi is of great value in the treatment of influenza, congestion of the lungs, asthma, chronic fever, dysmenorrhoea, and indigestion. In Bengal, *Vaidyas* treat leucorrhoea too with Tulsi preparations.

Tulsi seeds are ascribed highly nutritious qualities by Ayurveda.

Tulsi is gradually being accepted as a valuable therapeutic agent by modern science as well. Western scientists have come to believe as a result of a large number of investigations and tests that the Tulsi plant possesses extra electrical energy. This has the effect of keeping the air fresh and pure up to a distance of two hundred metres from a Tulsi plant. Even today in this scientific age one finds that many knowledgeable Englishmen cultivate the Tulsi plants all around their homes. There is a tradition of placing Tulsi leaves in foods and drinks that have to be stored during solar and lunar eclipse. The tradition is based on the fact that Tulsi leaves have bacteriocidal properties. The electrical energy of the leaves prevents the deleterious rays of the eclipsed luminaries from having an effect on the stored victuals. Charak and Sushrut in their treatises have given the appellation 'Surasa' or 'Suras' to Tulsi, to indicate the beneficent qualities of its juice. As it is easily available in every village, it is extensively used in the treatment of malaria, congestion of the lungs, cough, colitis, etc. Tulsi juice is applied as a first-aid measure to the bites and stings of poisonous insects and reptiles such as scorpions and snakes to reduce the effects of the poisons. It is believed that Tulsi juice has the capacity to neutralise the poisonous effects of mercury in the body.

A few years ago the Gujarat Government bestowed state honours on Dr. Upendrarai, a learned physician of Ahmadabad, for his researches on the medicinal properties of Tulsi, and his development of methods of treatment based on these qualities of Tulsi. Dr. Upendrarai believes that there is an unequalled capacity in Tulsi leaves to cure cancer, heart disease, and diseases of the kidneys and the skin. He asserts that treatment of mentally retarded children with Tulsi results in noticeable improvement in just fifteen days.

Tulsi grows abundantly not only in India, but also in many other countries, including Shreelanka, Burma, China, Malaya, Africa, Brazil, etc. Camphor can be extracted from the Tulsi plant. The Tulsi plants in America contain a smaller proportion of camphor. The plant yields a fragrant volatile oil too. The light-coloured variety of Tulsi contains up to 70 per cent of such oil.

It is said that the Muslims too have a tradition of placing Tulsi leaves in graves, as they are well aware of the importance of the therapeutic properties of Tulsi.

Tulsi is used in Brazil in the treatment of disorders of the rectum, the urinary system and the penis, as an infallible remedy. In Mauritius the bodies of people suffering from paralysis and rheumatoid disorders are traditionally washed with a hot decoction of Tulsi. Steam from such a decoction is used for the fomentation of diseased organs. It is in acknowledgement of these miraculous qualities of Tulsi that the Israelis use Tulsi in their religious ritual worship on various occasions such as marriage ceremonies, funeral ceremonies, and religious and social celebrations. All these facts prove that Tulsi is accorded a place of great importance and used with reverence and faith in religious ceremonies and medicinal applications not only in India but also in other countries.

A large number of many wonderful discoveries regarding its curative properties made since very ancient times have resulted in the adoption of Tulsi by itself and in conjunction with other medicines as a remedy for various diseases. The use of Tulsi has proved beneficial in the Ayurvedic treatment of numerous diseases such as fevers, sprains, piles, cataract, rheumatism, asthma, diarrhoea, eye diseases, tooth decay, pyorrhoea, burning sensation in the stomach, excessive thirst, toxaemia, scabies, eczema, pruritus, acne, catarrh, nocturnal emissions, leucorrhoea, syphilis, bladder stones, vomiting, coughs, loss of appetite, plague, hiccups, leprosy, jaundice, prickly heat, burns, burns caused by lightning, snake-bites, stings of scorpions, poisoning, loss of hair, labour pains, etc.

Modern chemists, too, are carrying out extensive investigations on this plant endowed with miraculous qualities. They have succeeded in isolating a substance from it which arrests the growth of the tuberculosis bacillus. According to reports published by the Vallabhbhai Patel Vriksha Sansthan, Delhi, an oily substance found in Tulsi actively destroys those bacilli.

The Imperial Malarial Conference has declared Tulsi to be a genuine remedy for malaria. Dr. Owen reports on the basis of his experience and investigations that Tulsi has astonishing powers of developing the body and ridding it of alien organisms. It has adequate antipyretic properties and a soothing action on the throat, thus relieving coughs. Sir George Woodward has described the anti-malarial property of Tulsi.

Tulsi has proved beneficial not only physically but also spiritually. Tulsi is 'Satvik', possessing spiritually uplifting qualities. People with a devotional bent of mind therefore wear strings of Tulsi beads around their necks, believing that it symbolises religious inclinations. Such Tulsi bead strings are essential adjuncts to rituals undertaken with the purpose of spiritual upliftment, and the use of these strings of Tulsi beads in such rituals has proved greatly conducive to mental peace. It helps in the elimination of the baser instincts. The holy water distributed in temples as 'charanamrit', which contains Tulsi leaves, has been observed to pacify minds excited by choleric or libidinous passions. Tulsi leaves are also added to 'panchamrit', the sweet liquid offered to God in prayer. Partaking of panchamrit as 'prasad' induces peace in the mind, humility in general behaviour, and sweetness in speech and tone. Wherever the wind that has touched Tulsi plants blows, sacred thoughts arise, spiritual upliftment prevails, and godliness fills the mind. It is only because of these ennobling qualities that Tulsi occupies a very lofty position in the spiritual world.

These days large members of posh sanatoria are erected on remote mountains, and people suffering from grave diseases like tuberculosis are advised to go and live in them. But the poor are not in a position to accept such advice, and to act in accordance with it. If 'Tulsi sanatoria' are set up in every town and every village, people in every walk of life can benefit from them. A large number of Tulsi plants should be grown in some suitable piece of land. Huts can be constructed in scattered places on this land, with materials like bamboos and grass. The soil from the Tulsi plot can be used to plaster the walls and the floors of these huts. A patient living in such a hut will breathe the salubrious air of the Tulsi garden. He will get the benefit of the fragrant essential oils released by the Tulsi plants into the atmosphere. The wind blowing through the Tulsi shrubs will help his lungs to regain health and strength, and his circulation to become normal. As a result, each cell of his body will regain health, the body will acquire fresh vigour and vitality, rid itself of even supposedly incurable diseases, and attain a state of perfect health. A stay in a Tulsi sanatorium coupled with Tulsi-based medicines will effect a complete cure at a very moderate expense.

Affluent philanthropists with the welfare of the people at heart should set up 'Tulsi-vans' in the land around their bungalows, and permit everyone suffering from an illness to have free access to the Tulsi plants.

The fragrant qualities of Tulsi have been described in detail in almost all scriptures. Numerous artificial and harmful perfumes are being extensively used these days. But in the remote past, only such substances were used as perfumes which were salubrious as well as fragrant, and which had no harmful effect on the body or the mind. From this point of view, Tulsi must surely be considered as occupying the topmost position among plants. That is why it was freely used to flavour items of food and drink. We are accustomed to flavouring vegetables by boiling spices with a little oil or ghee and then adding vegetables to the boiling mixture. In place of cumin seeds and other spices used in this process at present, the juice of Tulsi leaves was used in ancient times to impart an appetising flavour to foods. Tulsi leaves were also used to flavour rice and pullao in place of the dried tamal leaves we use today, though the use of Tulsi leaves in such preparations has continued in some regions. Even *kheer, halwa* and such other sweets are flavoured with Tulsi leaves in some places. Shyam Tulsi, because of its stronger aroma, is used to a greater extent in such preparations. The Europeans use Tulsi to improve the taste and aroma of wines and sauces. We Indians too should begin to use Tulsi freely in our daily diet to take full advantage of its medicinal properties.

The issue of 'Gujarat Samachar' dated 25-3-'88 carried a report from the PTI to the effect that research has proved Tulsi to be a health-giving plant par excellence. The report states further that "a study undertaken at the S. V. University, Tirupati, has established that the Tulsi plant exhales ozone, the molecules of which contain three atoms of oxygen, in place of the ordinary atmospheric oxygen, which has only two atoms of oxygen in each molecule."

The leaves of the Tulsi plant contain ether, which enables them to destroy bacteria, and drive away mosquitoes.

Shri Shobhanji, the renowned *vaidya*, has extolled the virtues of Tulsi in a wonderful poetic style. Here is a free translation of the poem :

With sharp taste and bitter aftertaste,
Hot, light and dry in effect,
It cures ailments originating in
kapha and vayu,
It stimulates hunger and
improves digestion,
It sharpens the intellect and
grants spiritual ennoblement,
It improves vision and
benefits the heart,
It imparts flavour and
disseminates fragrance.

"Tulsi is used in the treatment of fevers caused by *kapha* and *vayu*, colds, coughs, laboured breathing, pains, lack of appetite, slack digestion, crepitation, vomiting, hiccups, migraine, poisoning, headaches, sore throat, suppuration of the ears, skin diseases, flatulence, toothache, tetanus, dyspepsia, excessive thirst, urticaria, halitosis, cholera, smallpox, worms, chest pains, night blindness, liver disorders, etc."

● ● ●

The well-known Naturopath Shri Kartikeya Mahadevia states :

"Weight is reduced by taking Tulsi leaves with curds or buttermilk. The loss of fats improves the figure and makes the body well-proportioned and shapely. Fatigue is not experienced, and one feels energetic all day. The amount of haemoglobin in the blood increases, which prevents other diseases. The powers of the body to resist diseases develop to such an extent that minor ailments and even malaria, influenza and such other diseases cannot attack it. If during travels, especially during travel in foreign countries, Tulsi plants are not available to supply our needs, one can use dried and powdered Tulsi leaves. These are, of course, invaluable, but the cost price may be considered to be around Rs. 200 per kilogramme. An amount of the powder equivalent to ten to twenty leaves should be taken with curds or buttermilk, as directed above in case of the green leaves. Similarly, 'Tulsi Sudhā', a drink prepared from Tulsi and jaggery ground together, should be taken in preference to other drinks. People suffering from acidity benefit by adding Tulsi to curds and buttermilk. Tulsi purifies the blood, and strengthens the powers of the body to resist diseases, and thus creates conditions which ensure that no disease will be able to attack the body. In this way, Tulsi confers benefits in all respects.

Tulsi is too hot for women, but the adverse effects of this quality of Tulsi can be reduced by taking only 2 to 5 mashed leaves with one glass of buttermilk or 2 to 4 grammes of curds. Women should therefore make it a point to take Tulsi with curds or buttermilk. In fact, they should take the maximum possible amounts of curds and buttermilk every day. Women should also exercise caution in the use of jaggery and honey, as these sweeteners are also 'hot' in their physiological effects. Dissolving jaggery in warm or cold water and stirring Tulsi paste and lemon juice into it yields a very pleasant-tasting and salubrious drink, known as 'Tulsi Sudhā'. This drink should normally be taken only by men, and more specifically only by those who find that it agrees with them. Persons troubled by 'heat' in the physiological sense would be well advised to abstain from taking this drink.

> **TULSI DECLARED WONDER DRUG BY FRENCH DOCTOR**
>
> The French physician, Dr. Victor Racine, currently on a visit to India, has stated in a lecture, one of a series arranged by the Department of Pharmacology, Benares Hindu University, that "Tulsi is a wonder drug. In addition to its proven efficacy in controlling blood pressure, regulating the digestive system and stimulating the production of red blood corpuscles, it has yielded extraordinary results in mental disorders as well. It has also been found highly effective in preventing malaria and other common intermittent and enteric fevers."
>
> **(Gujarat Samachar, Dt. 24-12-'88)**

2. TULSI : THE HOMEOPATHIC POINT OF VIEW

An unorthodox system of therapeutics like Homeopathy, too, has recognised the importance of Tulsi, and experiments have been carried out on healthy persons to ascertain its physiological action. As a result of these investigations, Tulsi has won an eminent position in the Homeopathic Materia Medica. Dr. William Boericke, M. D. of the University of California has given it the appellation 'Brazilian Alfavaca', and described its characteristics in these terms :

"Tulsi is useful in the treatment of disorders of women such as prolapse of the vagina, pain in the labia majora, chest pains, soreness in the breasts, itching and obesity, and especially disorders of the urino-genital system. Anal constriction, sharp pains in the ureters, acidic urine, malodorous and turbid urine, deepening of the reddish or yellowish tinge in the colour of urine, passing blood or pus in urine, bladder stones, soreness in the kidneys (especially in the right kidney), etc. are conditions in which treatment with Tulsi has been found to be beneficial."

In a major article in the "Heinemannian Gleanings", a journal published from Mumbai, describing the experimentally established characteristics of Tulsi, Dr. Sharad Chandra Ghosh has written with a certain sense of pride that "Tulsi is being successfully used in the treatment of pneumonia, typhoid, influenza, diseases of the chest, brain, skin, stomach, intestines, eyes, mouth, ears, throat, face, urinary tract, etc., as well as infantile diarrhoea, worms, pyrexia and fevers accompanying teething." In his monograph on "Drugs of Hindosthan", Dr. Ghosh narrates many of his successful experiences in the use of Tulsi.

According to Dr. Moore, the wild variety of Tulsi, 'Van Tulsi', is considered to be an important remedy for disorders of the urino-gentital system. It has been reported by the British Homeopathic Society that Dr. Clarke was able to cure two patients of urinary diseases by treatment with Tulsi.

Drs. Prakash Prasanna Bishwas, N. Sinha and N. C. Ghosh have carried out extensive testing of this plant. Dr. Moore was the first to use Arjak Tulsi in Homeopathic treatment. This variety of Tulsi has come to be accepted as a specific remedy for disorders of the urinary system. Arjak Tulsi has also been found to be beneficial in prolapse of the vagina and soreness in the breasts of breast-feeding mothers.

'Ram Tulsi' is generally used for the treatment of constipation and similar conditions, especially when children have coughs, colds and fever along with constipation. This variety of Tulsi is particularly efficacious in gonorrhoeal dysuria, with pus being passed with urine.

'Marva' Tulsi, too, is widely used in cases of gonorrhoea and of semen passing with urine. It has a beneficial effect on the kidneys and the urinary system. It is, therefore, used to treat conditions like uremia, inflammation of the kidneys, retention of urine and the initial stages of gonorrhoea, characterized by excessive urination accompanied by a burning sensation, with pus in the urine.

Thus Tulsi is used in the treatment of a large number of disorders in the Homeopathic system as well.

Important Warning : If Tulsi juice is to be warmed, absolutely no honey should be mixed with it. Honey must never be warmed, or mixed with hot substances. Warmed honey is toxic. As far as possible, aged honey should be used in medicinal applications and fresh honey for nutritional and invigorating action. Aged honey has a moderating effect on the three humours *vata, pitta* and *kapha,* whereas fresh honey stimulates the secretion of the humours.

Contraindications : Persons with constitutions having a 'hot' physiological tendency, persons suffering from diseases of such a nature, or with a tendency to bleed, or with an excessive susceptibility to heat, should never take Tulsi in any form in the Greeshma and Sharad seasons (May-June and September-October). Nor should Tulsi be taken with betel leaves in the month of Kartik (which overlaps with November). Those suffering from piles should avoid taking Tulsi and black pepper together, as this combination is likely to prove excessively hot.

Milk taken with all fruits, all sour foods, meat, garlic, onions, salt, radishes, carrots, jaggery or Tulsi has a deleterious effect.

3. TULSI : THE AYURVEDIC POINT OF VIEW

Tulsi in Major Ayurvedic Works

(1) Shree Aryabhishak : Tulsi is grown in front of the dwellings of all Hindus, and is deemed to be a very holy plant among Hindus. The Tulsi plant grows to the height of approximately two to four feet (60 to 120 cms.). There are two main varieties of Tulsi, the light and the dark varieties, recognised by the colour of the leaves. The leaves of one variety are rather dark in colour, while those of the other variety are bright green. Tulsi bears clusters of flowers (inflorescences), in which seeds are formed. These inflorescences (or *manjaris*) and Tulsi leaves are used in devotional offerings during pooja worship of gods and goddesses. The leaves and seeds possess a characteristic aroma. Some medicinal preparations are subjected to the process of *bhavna* with the help of Tulsi juice. 'Marva' is also a variety of Tulsi, with qualities similar to those of Tulsi. The darker variety of Tulsi is superior in its medicinal properties to the lighter-coloured variety.

In view of the unrivalled qualities of Tulsi, our ancient sages have with great foresight recommended that there should be a Tulsi plant in the courtyard of every dwelling – a recommendation that reveals their perfect wisdom. A Tulsi plant in the courtyard promotes health. A certain gas emanating from the Tulsi plant destroys the deleterious substances in the surrounding air and thus purifies it. Our religion has prescribed the ritual of daily worship and circumambulation of the Tulsi plant. That this is of great benefit to us is a fact that needs no emphasis. The creation of numerous plants with beneficent qualities, such as Tulsi possesses, for the benefit of our countrymen, is a special boon conferred by God on us. For maintaining the purity of the atmosphere in our homes, these plants should be reared in pots, and one or two of these pots should be placed during the day in every room and every part of our homes in daily use. In the evenings, these pots should be carried out into the open, and left there overnight, to be brought back into the house in the morning and arranged as before. This will ensure the house in the morning and arranged as before. This will ensure the maintenance of the health of everyone in the family, and prevent disorders arising from excesses of humours such as *vayu*. Tulsi is slightly bitter, hot, sharp in taste, fragrant and stimulator of appetite. It destroys *vayu, kapha,* swellings, worms and a tendency to vomit. Both the lighter and the darker varieties of Tulsi are pungent in taste, hot in physiological action, sharp, causing a burning sensation, promoting the secretion of *pitta,* beneficial to the heart, somewhat bitter, stimulating the digestive organs, and easy to digest. Both of them destroy *vayu,* asthma, cough, hiccups, worms, vomiting, bad odours, leucoderma, pain in the flanks, toxins, dysuria, abnormalities of the blood, harassment by evil spirits, pains, fevers and spasms. They are used in the treatment of fevers, disinclination to work, lassitude, lack of appetite, burning sensation, abnormalities of *vata* and *pitta*.

Preparations : *(1)* Laghuraajamriganka, *(2)* Tulsi Taila (Oil).

(1) Laghuraajamriganka : This is prepared by mixing equal proportions of Tulsi juice, ghee prepared from cow's milk, and pepper.

(2) Tulsi Taila : This is prepared by taking equal proportions of Tulsi leaf paste, the roots of *bhoringani* plant, *danti* roots, *vaj,* bark of the drumstick tree, dry (stone) ginger, pepper, *piper longum,* and saindhav salt, adding *til* (seasame) oil four times the combined weight of the above ingredients, and water sixteen times the combined weight of the ingredients, and letting the oil mature.

Qualities : Destroyer of *kapha,* hot in action.

Uses : Tulsi leaves are useful in the treatment of excessive phlegm, coughs and pain in the flanks. Tulsi is used to get rid of the excessive amounts of phlegm that accumulate in some kinds of coughs. Tulsi is also generally used to reinforce the medicines given in the treatment of the excessive accumulation of phlegm in the lungs of children, and in the treatment of adults for coughs, asthma, laboured breathing, etc. As Tulsi possesses the quality of being *'ushnaveerya'*, increasing the vitality of the body, it can be administered with advantage in all disorders caused by excess of *vayu* in the body. In the treatment of *vatajwara* (influenza), Tulsi is usually mixed with other medicines. This results in reducing somnolence, and thus reducing the soporific effects. The patient stops murmuring incoherently in a semi-conscious condition, and regains consciousness. Tulsi is used less frequently by itself, but much more extensively as *anupaan*, i.e., as a salubrious addendum to other medicines to reinforce their action. It is an appetiser and so promotes appetite. It cures colic, flatulence, and gas in the stomach. Toothache can be cured by pressing a paste of crushed ginger enfolded in two or three Tulsi leaves on either side, with the aching teeth. This treatment with a piece of ginger and Tulsi leaves is very effective in the treatment of toothache, whether due to cavities in the teeth or to any other reason. Tulsi is the *anupaan* generally prescribed to reinforce the action of medicines given in cases of spasms. Tulsi juice taken with pepper powder is beneficial in typhoid fever. All disorders caused by *vayu* are cured by treatment with the Tulsi preparation *'Laghuraajamriganka'* mentioned above. This also enhances the glow of the body. Lesions in the nostrils resulting in Ozena (Atrophic rhinitis) can be successfully treated by inhaling dried powdered Tulsi leaves. Decay in the nasal passages is cured by instilling Tulsi *Taila* into the nostrils.

Dose : Juice 20 grammes;

Laghuraajamriganka 10 grammes.

(2) Sushrut Ayurveda : The variety of Tulsi that bears white inflorescences and has bright green leaves is a destroyer of *kapha, vayu,* toxins, asthma, coughs and bad odours. It stimulates the secretion of *pitta,* and relieves pain in the flanks. The wild variety of Tulsi also possesses these qualities, and is especially effective in destroying toxins.

The variety of Tulsi that bears dark inflorescences, and the two other varieties known as *'kshudra'* Tulsi and *'Bhoostrina'* are all destroyers of *kapha*. They are easily digestible, dry and somewhat *snigdha*, mild and ameliorating. They are also *'ushnaveerya'*, increasing the vitality of the body; they promote the secretion of *pitta* and are sharp in effect and taste.

(3) Traditional Homely Therapeutics : It has already been explained that *'anupaan'* implies salubrious accompaniments or addenda to medicines which help to reinforce and increase the efficacy of other medicines. A list of *anupaans* for various disorders is being given below.

Fevers – 1. Tea (decoction) prepared from Tulsi and *bilwa* leaves; 2. Decoction prepared from Tulsi leaves, *bilwa* leaves and dry ginger; 3. Decoction of Tulsi leaves; 4. Tulsi leaf juice and honey.

Typhoid fever – 1. Tulsi juice; 2. Mixed juices of ginger and Tulsi.

Excess of *Kapha* and Asthma – Tulsi juice and crystal sugar.

Diabetes – *Bangabhasma* and Tulsi leaves.

Excessive *Vayu* – *Pravālabhasma* (calcined coral), honey or crystal sugar, and Tulsi juice; pure sulphur, Tulsi juice and *ghee*.

Night Blindness – *Pravālabhasma* and the droppings of mice should be ground with honey, and the resulting paste should be applied, like an ointment, to the eyes.

Tulsi : The Tulsi plants grow wild in all sorts of land and climates. They are also grown in gardens, and Hindus with a religious inclination grow the plants in pots or in the courtyards of their homes. Small dark seeds, smaller than those *of tukmariya* or of mustard, are formed in the inflorescences. There are two main varieties of Tulsi : 1. Krishna Tulsi – so named because of the darker colour of its twigs and leaves. 2. Shweta or Ram Tulsi – the leaves and the stem and twigs of which are green in colour. The medicinal virtues of both are the same.

Medicinal Virtues : 1. Hot in effect, sharp in taste, stimulator of appetite, useful in the treatment of excess of *vayu*, asthma, coughs, hiccups, vomiting, worms, toxins, harassment due to evil spirits and micro-organisms, fevers and spasms. 2. Decoction (tea) of Tulsi leaves about 10 grammes of Tulsi leaves boiled in 50 grammes of water till half or three quarters of the water has been boiled away yields a decoction, which on drinking will cure fevers, lassitude, lack of appetite, burning sensation, and will counter the effects of excessive formation of *vayu* or *pitta*. Apparently the tradition of growing the Tulsi plants in every home is based on these medicinal virtues. Tulsi also destroys toxins. Many disorders of the body can be cured and the body nourished and strengthened by regularly drinking a decoction of Tulsi (Tulsi tea) with some milk, sugar and cardamom.

Preparation : Tulsi leaf juice should be taken with powdered pepper seeds.

(4) Bhavprakāsh : Various appellations of the dark and light varieties of Tulsi – Tulasi, surasā, grāmyā, sulabhā, bahumanjari, apetaraakshasi gauri, shoolaghni and devadundubhi are some of the Sanskrit appellations of Tulsi, each one of which is significant.

1. One that has no equal, bears or tolerates no comparison, and so is beyond comparison – Tulasi.

2. The rasa or juice of which is best – Surasā.

3. One that flourishes in open land especially in village areas – Grāmyā.

4. One that can be obtained easily – Sulabhā.

5. One that bears many clusters of flowers, or inflorescences *(manjaris)* – Bahumanjari.

6. One from whose sight rākshasas and sins (which share the evil nature of rākshasas) flee Apetaraakshasi.

7. The fair one, the light-coloured one (describing the lighter-coloured variety of Tulsi) – Gauri.

8. One that destroys (kills) pain – Shoolaghni.

9. One that gives pleasure to the gods, and so is as pleasure-giving as the dundubhi drums – Devadundubhi.

Qualities of the Shyama – Shweta varieties of Tulsi : Tulsi is sharp and bitter in taste, beneficial to the heart, hot in physiological effect and stimulator of the digestive system. It therefore cures burning sensations, excess of *pitta,* leucoderma, dysuria, toxaemia, pain in the flanks, excess of *kapha* and *vayu.* Both the lighter-coloured and darker varieties are similar in their medicinal virtues.

The appellations and qualities of the Barbari variety of Tulsi : Barbari, Tuvari, Tungi, Kharapushpā, Ajagandhikā and Parsnāsa are the Sanskrit appellations of Barbari Tulsi. But the darker variety of Barbari Tulsi is known as Kathinjar or Kutherak. The lighter-coloured variety of Barbari Tulsi is known as Arjak. There is a third variety of Barbari Tulsi, which is known as Vatapatra. All the three varieties are dry, cool in effect and bitter in taste, cause a burning sensation, are sharp, stimulate appetite, are beneficial to the heart, increase the powers of digestion, are easy to digest and stimulate the production of *pitta.* These varieties of Tulsi are therefore effective in curing excess of *kapha, vata,* toxaemia, itching and worms. They are also good antidotes for poisons.

The significance of the various names of the Barbari varieties of Tulsi is explained below :

1. One that accepts a large variety of different kinds of virtues – Barbari.

2. One whose juice is somewhat bitter, or one that destroys *kapha, vayu* and toxins – Tuvari.

3. One that destroys poisons, or one that grows to a great height – Tungi.

4. One that bears rough, hard flower clusters – Kharapushpā.

5. One that possesses a smell resembling that of goats – Ajagandhikā.

6. One that sheds leaves, or that has a beauteous appearance because of leaves – Parnāsa.

7. One that helps the digestion of even hard materials because of its sharpness and capacity to stimulate digestion – Kathinjar, the darker variety of Barbari Tulsi.

8. One that destroys *kapha, vayu,* etc. – Kutherak, the darker variety of Barbari Tulsi.

9. One that confers or acquires a fair complexion – Arjak, the lighter-coloured variety of Barbari Tulsi.

10. One whose leaves resemble the leaves of the banyan tree – Vatapatra, the third variety of Barbari Tulsi.

"Any major disease that has penetrated into the skin, the flesh or the bones is eliminated by Rama (White) Tulsi. Shyama Tulsi is a beautifier, eliminating all skin diseases, restoring the skin to its normal and natural state. Tulsi is wonderfully beneficial for the skin." (Atharvaveda)

•

"Tulsi is bitter and sharp in taste, beneficial to the heart, hot in action, causes a burning sensation, promotes the secretion of bile and stimulates appetite. It cures leprosy, dysuria, toxaemia, and pain in the flanks, and destroys *kapha* and *vata.* Both the white and the dark varieties are medicinally of equal merit." (Bhavamishra)

•

"Tulsi cures hiccups, coughs, toxaemia, laboured breathing and pain in the flanks. It promotes secretion of bile and destroys *vata, kapha* and bad breath."

(Charak Sootras 27, 169)

•

"Both the white and dark varieties of Tulsi are bitter and sharp in taste and hot in effect. They cause a burning sensation, stimulate the production of bile, and benefit the heart. They stimulate appetite, are easy to digest and destroy *kapha,* respiratory disorders, coughs, hiccups and worms. They cure vomiting, bad odours, leprosy, pain in the flanks, effects of toxins, dysuria, toxaemia, harassment due to evil spirits, pains, fevers and hiccups." (Nighanturatnakar)

"Tulsi is bitter and sharp, stimulates appetite, destroys *kapha* and *vata*, and kills minute organisms."
(Rajnighantu 10, 158)

"Wherever the aroma of Tulsi is carried by the wind, it purifies the atmosphere and frees all animals from all baser tendencies." (Padmapurana, Uttarkhanda)

"Every home with a Tulsi plant is a place of pilgrimage, and no diseases, messengers of yama, the God of Death, can enter it."
(Skandapurana, 2, 4, 8, 13; Padmapurana, Uttarkhanda)

"Habitual use of Tulsi cures headaches, nasal catarrh, migraine, epilepsy, and nasal disorders."

"Tulsi has healing and curative properties. It destroys *vata*, worms and foul odour. It has the capacity to overcome disorders like dryness, coughs, laboured breathing, lack of appetite and pain in the ribs." (Rajavallabh)

"Tulsi is light, hot, neutralises *kapha*, cures disorders caused by worms, stimulates appetite and promotes digestion."
(Dhanvantarinighantu)

"Tulsi neutralises *vata* and *kapha*, eases laboured breathing, cures coughs, vomiting, disorders caused by worms, and destroys foul odours. It is beneficial in leprosy, pains in the ribs, toxaemia and disorders of the eyes." (Kaiy. 1129)

"Tulsi is bitter, sharp in taste and hot in its action. It destroys worms and micro-organisms. It conquers *kapha* and *vata*. It stimulates digestion. It is dry, stimulates appetite and is helpful in vomiting."

•

"Tulsi prevents untimely death (confers longevity) and destroys all kinds of disorders."

•

"When the ocean was churned by Lord Vishnu to obtain *amrit*, among the medicinal herbs which he created for the welfare of all living things the first one to be created was Tulsi."

•

"No servants of Yama can retain a footing in a house where there is water and soil sanctified by Tulsi. That is to say, in houses where water and soil which have been in contact with Tulsi are used, disease germs cannot thrive."

•

"Vegetables prepared from Kathinjar (Krishna Tulsi) leaves are heavy, difficult to digest, and cause dryness and constipation. But if the vegetables are prepared by first boiling the leaves, squeezing them to remove excess fluids, and then sauteing them in plenty of ghee, it is soothing in taste and effect, makes the semen milder and relieves constipation."
(Charak, sootras 27-99, 103, 104)

•

"Vegetables prepared by cooking Barbari and Arjak (Kutherak) Tulsi are bitter, make the semen milder, possess the beneficial effects of bitterness, and neutralize *kapha* and *pitta*."
(Charak, sootras 27-96, 98)

•

"Vishnu, the Lord of the Three Worlds, takes up abode in the village or the house where Tulsi is grown. In such a house no one suffers calamities like poverty, illness or separation from dear ones."

(Padmapurana, Uttarkhanda, 6-24-31-32)

4. TULSI : TESTED THERAPEUTIC APPLICATIONS

Tulsi is described as the 'immortality herb'. Though this claim is a bit exaggerated, it cannot be denied that Tulsi is a herb that confers longevity. Its therapeutic use proves miraculously successful. It plays a very important part in the elimination of various kinds of toxins, or poisons. The presence of poisons in the body is not merely due to stings of poisonous insects such as wasps and scorpions, or bites of snakes, monkeys, rabid dogs, etc. (These are poisons that enter the body from outside.) But there are also poisons that are generated inside the body, and manifest themselves in the form of various disorders like furuncles, pustules, itching, cancer, malaria, cholera, etc. These poisons entering the blood-stream destroy the red blood corpuscles and contaminate the blood. This weakens the body and renders it vulnerable to various illnesses. Weakness is the mother of all diseases. Tulsi destroys the poisons generated in the body due to irregularity in food habits and life-style, lack of self-control and weakness, as well as the poisons that have entered the body through stings and bites. If Tulsi-based medication is used with due regard to the prescribed manner of administration, it is sure to yield miraculous results.

Most major and minor illnesses yield readily to treatment with Tulsi. Some specific cases are described here, which will throw light on the efficacy of Tulsi and enable us to appreciate its virtues better.

* **Naturophathic Regulations in Uruliknchan Ashram founded by Mahatma Gandhi :** The inmates of the Ashram are not permitted to take tea, coffee, sugar, etc. For those among the inmates who have been in the habit of taking tea etc., a decoction of Tulsi, ginger and the fragrant herb known as green tea is prepared in the establishment. Treacle and milk are added to the decoction, which is then served to the

tea-addicts. Instead of the harmful effects of tea, this Tulsi decoction has benefical effects on health.

* Tulsi increases the efficiency of the kidneys. In one instance, continuous treatment with Tulsi juice mixed with honey for six months was sufficient to rid the patient of kidney stones.

* After trying various treatments and even operating on a patient suffering from intra-tacheal cancer, his doctors lost all hope and declared that as the liver of the patient was being irreversibly damaged, and the tumour was growing rapidly, there was no hope of a cure. This conclusion was challenged by a *vaidya*. He started administering Tulsi regularly. After five weeks of this treatment the patient recovered sufficiently to be able to walk a mile !

* An aged woman was suffering from vaginal cancer. When radiotherapy with radium and cobalt failed to effect a cure, the doctors lost all hope. But after only ten days' treatment with Tulsi, the bleeding and the pain began to decrease, and stopped completely after a month. The mucous membrane became normal and the lesions healed !

* High blood pressure of many patients suffering from heart disease has been brought down to normal by treatment with Tulsi. Their hearts have been strengthened and their blood cholesterol levels have come down. Many of the patients who had been forbidden to go to hill stations have enjoyed very pleasant vacations in high-altitude resorts after regular treatment with Tulsi !

* An instance of the wonderful efficacy of Tulsi on snake-bite was reported in the periodical "Modern Review", published from Calcutta. An inhabitant of a remote village was bitten by a snake. No doctor or *vaidya* was able to reach the village for eight hours. When finally a *vaidya* did reach the place, the victim was lying unconscious. The *vaidya* crushed Tulsi leaves and squeezed out the juice. The juice was rubbed into the skin on the face, the forehead and the chest of the patient.

The juices of Tulsi leaves and the stem of a banana plant were mixed and given to the patient in 10 millilitre portions every few minutes. This treatment effected a complete cure. This very treatment was successfully tried in an Ashram of the Ramakrishna Mission.

* An interesting incident was reported by the wellknown physician Nalini Nath Mazumdar in a periodical called *"Chikitsa Prakash"*. One of his friends was to have electric wiring installed in his house. He went to the residence of the Chief Engineer of Calcutta City for discussions in this connection. To his astonishment he saw that there were Tulsi plants being grown in pots all over the place. An Englishman decorating his bungalow by growing Tulsi plants instead of flowers and creepers ! Not being able to contain his curiosity, he questioned the engineer about this. And this was the reply : "That you are surprised at seeing Tulsi plants everywhere in my bungalow, surprises me even more. Though you are a Hindu, you are not aware of the great importance of Tulsi ! Extensive literature has been published in my country on Tulsi. Is there no book dealing with it in India ? The fact is, no other plant contains as much electrical energy as does Tulsi. All the air within a distance of 600 feet from a Tulsi plant is influenced by it. As a result, the micro-organisms causing malaria, plague, and T. B. are destroyed. I carry a Tulsi twig tied to my waist to protect myself from attack by disease germs. I take a stroll in a Tulsi garden every morning and evening, and in consequence enjoy excellent health."

* An article by Shri Vishwanath Prasad on the efficacy of Tulsi was published in the November 1940 issue of *'Jeevan Sakha'*. A friend of Shri Prasad, aged 35, was taken ill. Day by day he became weaker and weaker, and lost weight. Treatment by numerous doctors and *vaidyas* proved of no avail. Ultimately he was brought to the Government Hospital in Patna. The doctors declared that his liver had deteriorated. They prescribed cod-liver oil and other costly medicines. These were also tried, but there was no improvement. His disease was pronounced incurable. The members of his family were in despair. Everyone took it as final that his end was near. He decided, in accordance with Hindu beliefs, to spend the rest of his days in the lap of Mother Ganga. As luck would have it, saintly Mahatma happened to come to their village in the course of his travels, at this time. He inquired about this man's illness, and ascertained the nature of the symptoms and other relevant details. He then instructed the patient to take Tulsi and the holy water of the Ganga on an empty stomach every morning. These instructions were carried out. The disease that had been declared incurable by *vaidyas* and doctors was cured within a month, and has not recurred so far!

* An old man was suffering from three serious diseases : asthma, colitis and leucocytosis (an increase in the number of leucocytes in the blood). His intestines too had become diseased. But Tulsi treatment effected an extremely rapid improvement.

* A seven-year old girl was allergic to drugs. The ingestion of any drug would cause bluish spots to appear all over her body, and her blood would get thinner. Numerous remedies were tried, but in vain. Only when regular treatment with Tulsi was instituted could this allergy be finally eradicated.

* A man of mature age, who had been suffering from allergic colds from the time of his birth, was completely cured by treatment with Tulsi.

* A young man used to have attacks of fever every month, each attack lasting for six to seven days. He took Tulsi decoction regularly for three months. There was absolutely no recurrence of the fever after that.

* A man had been suffering from headaches for fifteen years. Regular treatment with Tulsi enabled him to free himself from this affliction.

* A boy was mentally retarded from his childhood. Various treatments were tried for sixteen years, but there was no benefit. After regular treatment with Tulsi was instituted, signs of intellectual development were exhibited in only two months. With the passage of time the boy became very intelligent.

* A young man troubled by sinusitis was advised by doctors to undergo an operation. He was prepared for that. But on the advice of a *vaidya* he tried Tulsi treatment for two weeks. His cold and other symptoms disappeared, and he was saved from the necessity of having to undergo surgery.

* The kidney stones of a patient disintegrated and were flushed out of the system by treatment with Tulsi for six months. In this case the patient was given pure honey with Tulsi, as curds, which would normally be given with Tulsi, did not agree with him.

* Many persons who had leucoderma have derived marvellous benefits from treatment with Tulsi. The white spots have faded and the skin has acquired its normal colour.

* Tulsi has proved helpful in the treatment of disorders of the prostate too.

These instances make it clear that Tulsi can help us in getting rid of many incurable and painful diseases including cancer.

There have been numerous cases where Tulsi has proved successful even when doctors had failed.

Some tried and tested remedial procedures involving the use of Tulsi are given here. Note them in your diaries and use them as occasions arise.

(1) If diluted juice of Tulsi leaves is taken on an empty stomach every morning, it helps in the development of bodily strength, memory and an impressive personality. Drinking Tulsi decoction with a little sugar and cow's milk gives energy and removes fatigue. Daily ingestion of Tulsi juice maintains the digestive efficiency of the stomach and promotes appetite. If

Tulsi juice with a little salt in it is dropped into the nostrils of an unconscious person, the person quickly regains consciousness. The same mixture is effective in curing hiccups too.

(2) Tulsi quickly reduces blood cholesterol to normal levels. Daily use of Tulsi removes acidity, cures dysentery, colitis, etc. and is very beneficial in muscular pain, colds, leucoderma, obesity, headaches, etc. It is a very effective remedy for some disorders of children, particularly colds, diarrhoea, vomiting and congestion due to *kapha*. The use of Tulsi is astonishingly beneficial in heart disease and the weakness and other ailments incidental to it.

(3) Tulsi is equally beneficial in diseases of men, women and children. And its chief merit is that its use is always beneficial, and causes absolutely no adverse effects.

(4) Knowledge of the remedies for various diseases is traditionally passed down from generation to generation through sayings embodied in couplets and verses. In many of these one finds indications of the therapeutic virtues of Tulsi, ginger, garlic, radishes, bottle gourd and other herbs and vegetables, as also advice about good habits of eating and drinking. In one such traditional composition, this is what has been said about Tulsi :

If one takes Tulsi seeds daily with betel leaves, the amounts of blood and semen will increase and impotence will be cured.

If eleven Tulsi leaves are taken with four black pepper seeds, malaria, periodic fever and all other ailments will be cured.

(5) If regularity in food habits and life-style is not observed, many disorders of *vata* may result, one of which is *gradhrasivata*, characterised by pain in one of the nerves of the body. Pain similar to that caused by a sharp object is experienced in the hip joints, waist, back, abdomen, thighs or feet. There may be frequent attacks of trembling in the hip joints. The pain may occur at any location from the waist to the feet.

If steam from boiling water containing Tulsi leaves is used for fomentation of the affected part, much relief is obtained.

(6) Elderly people who have been taking Tulsi regularly do not experience the weakness that is generally associated with old age. On the contrary, they are full of energy and enthusiasm, and possess considerably greater powers of resistance to diseases.

(7) The mode of treatment with Tulsi is extremely simple. Five to seven leaves are sufficient for children, while adults require 25 to 100 leaves, depending upon their constitutions, their capacities, the disorders and the seasons (more leaves being necessary in winter than in summer). The leaves are ground to a paste on a clean flat stone and the juice is squeezed out. Five to ten millilitres of this juice can be given at a time, according to the constitution of the patient. About a gramme of the inflorescences (clusters of flowers, manjari) of Tulsi can be given with the juice. The inflorescences clear the urine and have an invigorating effect on the body. If fresh leaves cannot be obtained, dried and powdered leaves can be used instead.

(8) Tulsi-based medicines should normally be taken only once a day in the early morning on an empty stomach, after the daily morning bodily functions. A daily morning dose of two to three spoonfuls of Tulsi-leaf juice taken on an empty stomach helps to develop bodily strength, memory and an impressive personality. In case of relatively greater discomfort, the juice can be taken two or three times in a day.

(9) Those who want to liberate themselves from addiction to tea and tobacco etc. should change over to Tulsi decoction as a substitute for these intoxicants. They should also make it a practice to chew Tulsi leaves with black pepper. Such use of Tulsi has been known to help even alcoholics in freeing themselves from their addiction.

(10) Tulsi becomes even more efficacious when its use is accompanied by Yogic asanas and breath-control exercises. Naturopathic and Homeopathic treatments too are more effective when supplemented by Tulsi therapy. Because Tulsi is very dear to Lord Vishnu, the therapeutic value of Tulsi is increased manifold if one concentrates reverently on God while taking it. Those who take Tulsi with such an humble and devotional attitude derive miraculous benefits.

(11) Each of the parts of the Tulsi plant such as the leaves, seeds and twigs possesses medicinal properties. Its roots reduce the virulence of fevers. Its seeds thicken the semen (confer virility) and possess extraordinary powers of increasing the efficiency of digestive organs.

(12) Whether one wants to lose weight or to gain weight, Tulsi is equally beneficial, helping to develop a healthy and well-proportioned body. Tulsi has proved to be an infallible remedy for poor digestion, lack of appetite, constipation, flatulence, acidity and other disorders of the digestive tract.

5. TULSI : THE BEAUTIFIER

Everyone likes to look, and to keep looking, beautiful and attractive. Human beings are constantly worried about the preservation of the good looks with which Nature has endowed them. Beauty is directly dependent on health. Nature has therefore given us a large variety of medicinal herbs and shrubs to preserve health and beauty. Among these, Tulsi holds an important position.

Tulsi possesses two very useful virtues : promoting health and enhancing beauty. As it has bacteriocidal properties, it has had the reputation, from the most ancient times, of being a bestower of health and beauty. The importance that religion has attached to Tulsi is due entirely to these two superb qualities. Its health-giving and beautifying powers are unrivalled.

Early in the morning, after your bath, spread a mat in the proximity of a Tulsi plant, and sit in such a position as to allow the fragrance emanating from its leaves, inflorescences and stem to mix with the air you inhale and to fill your entire being with ecstasy. Inhale deeply, and hold your breath. Let the maximum amount of the fragrance enter your lungs with the air inhaled through the nostrils. Let this fragrant air laden with salubrious chemicals penetrate your body as deeply as possible. Let it pervade every drop of your blood. This divine aroma will purify your blood. The purified blood will impart a glow to your body and give it new life. This fragrance is very effective in increasing the beauty, health and radiance of the body. It has a great capacity of purifying the blood and correcting any unfavourable alteration in it. Your body will acquire glow and your face will become radiant. Your beauty will thus be greatly enhanced.

Tulsi is considered the best remedy for leucoderma and other skin disorders.

Rubbing finely powdered dry Tulsi leaves on the face like talcum powder makes it glow with beauty. This powder will also remove light and dark spots on the face.

Tulsi leaves purify the blood. Chewing a few leaves of the plant will purify the blood and turn it bright red. This in itself will improve your looks. Again, applying a thick paste formed by crushing and grinding dry Tulsi with a little pure water to the face opens up the pores of the skin. The dirt in them is easily flushed out of the pores through perspiration, leaving the skin glowing, soft, clear, and free from odoriferous substances, thus imparting radiance to the face.

For natural freshness of the skin of the face, try this : Take some water in a vessel. Squeeze half a lemon into it. Now add a fistful of Tulsi leaves, a handful of mint leaves, and boil it. Now cover your hair and expose only your face to the steam emanating from this water. Apply some of the water to your face when it has cooled down to a bearable temperature.

If there are dark spots on your face, add some lemon juice to the juice of Tulsi leaves and apply this mixture on the spots. Let it dry, and then wash it off with clear water. If this is done regularly every morning and evening, the spots will disappear in a few days and the face will become clean, fresh and glowing. An equal amount of ginger juice can be substituted for the lemon juice.

A decoction of Tulsi and mint is an excellent rejuvenator.

Tulsi is also useful for treating acne.

Keep lemon juice for twenty-four hours in a copper vessel. Add the same amount of Tulsi juice and kasaundi juice. (The fruit known as kasaundi, or kasaunji or harfa revdi can be obtained from any perfumier.) Thicken the mixture by evaporating it in sunlight. Apply this paste to the face. Gradually the skin of your face will become clear, glowing and beautiful.

6. TREATMENT OF SNAKE-BITE, STINGS OF INSECTS AND OTHER POISONS

* In case of poisoning of the system through any agency, the maximum possible amount of Tulsi juice must be taken. This will help in neutralizing and deactivating the poison. If opium or any other poisonous material like datura or aconite has been inadvertently imbibed, give the patient a paste of Tulsi leaves mixed with ghee obtained from cow's milk. One hundred to five hundred grammes of ghee should be given in this manner, depending on the condition of the patient. If no improvement is noticed even after this treatment, a similar

quantity of the mixture should be administered at intervals, till the effects of the poison disappear.

* Gargling with Tulsi extract gives relief in mercury poisoning. Continued treatment with the extract will reduce the pain and the salivation caused by mercury.

* Administering 50 grammes of Tulsi juice every day will eliminate the effects of calomel (hartal) poisoning in a week.

* There are allusions to the antidotal action of Tulsi against various poisons in ancient works on Ayurveda. Here is an extract from Charak-samhita :

"In case of snake-bite, a paste obtained by grinding together seeds of aconite, Tulsi, indrayan, satodi, piludi and black saras should be applied to the bite, a few drops of it should be introduced into the nostrils, and the patient made to swallow some of it."

* A paste of crushed Tulsi leaves with butter or ghee obtained from cow's milk should be applied to the bite of a snake. The paste will gradually darken under the effect of the poison. The darkened paste should be washed off and fresh paste applied. Repetition of this procedure will draw out the poison. Giving the patient a fistful or two of Tulsi leaves to chew and swallow will help.

* The victim of a snake-bite should be asked to chew some seeds of Bubai-Barbari Tulsi. (The stem of this variety of Tulsi has a rough surface.) When the seeds have been chewed to a thin paste, the patient should swallow half of it, and the rest of it should be applied on the bite. Quick relief can be obtained by administering about 50 grammes of the juice of Tulsi leaves.

* The poison spreading from the bite of a snake can be rendered inactive by administering Tulsi leaf juice to the victim, dropping a little juice into the eyes and ears, and applying a paste obtained by crushing and grinding the roots of the plant at the location of the bite. A paste of the crushed inflorescences will also serve the purpose.

* Snake poison can be deactivated by administering every two hours a mixture obtained by crushing together 20 leaves of a Tulsi plant with 10 black pepper seeds.

* If the victim of a snake-bite has lost consciousness, incisions should be made on the crown of the head, and leaves of the dark variety of Tulsi put on the incisions with a bandage to hold them in place. The juice of crushed leaves can be substituted for the leaves. This treatment will counter the effects of the poison, and the patient will regain consciousness.

* If bitten by a snake, one should drink the juice obtained by crushing and grinding Tulsi, jatamansi, saffron, turmeric, red sandalwood, pure manashil, nakhi, tamal patra, cinnamon and tagar with sufficient water. The juice should also be dropped into the nose and the eyes. This will destroy the poison, and the swelling caused by the poison will subside.

* Applying the paste obtained by grinding roots of a Tulsi plant with a woman's breast milk to the eyes, in a manner similar to that of applying carbon black or *kajal,* and dropping some of this liquid into the nostrils, will bring immediate relief to a person who has lost consciousness due to the bite of a snake.

* If the victim of a snake-bite is sinking, and is in immediate danger of death, he should be given pills rolled from Tulsi, mulethi, powdered wood turmeric, kooth, turmeric and gopitta. The condition of the victim will improve.

* Applying the paste of Tulsi leaves and roots ground together on the sting of a scorpion will completely eliminate the effects of the poison.

* If stung by a scorpion, rub the paste of Tulsi leaves and inflorescences over the sting. Crush a few leaves of Tulsi with cow's urine and lemon juice, and apply the paste over the region of the sting like an embrocation. Apply Tulsi juice to which a little rock salt has been added. Chew some Tulsi leaves. Grind together 20 grammes of Tulsi leaves and

15 black pepper seeds with water, and apply the paste on the sting.

* The pain caused by the sting of a wasp can be relieved by drinking Tulsi juice and applying it on the sting.

* The poison of a rat is destroyed by applying a mixture of Tulsi juice and opium.

* The poison of a rat can also be destroyed by making incisions at the site of the bite with a sharp penknife and applying a paste obtained by rubbing a cow's tooth on a grindstone with Tulsi juice, mixing manashil with the paste, and applying the paste over the incisions.

* Relief can be obtained from the painful effects of the poison of the bite of a centipede by administering at intervals of every fifteen minutes, 50 grammes of Tulsi juice mixed with ghee obtained from cow's milk and 5 grammes of black pepper powder.

* The bite of a centipede should be treated by the application and internal administration of wine to which Tulsi, *shankhini,* mineral soda bicarb (saaji khar) and ashes obtained by burning the droppings of goats have been added.

* To get rid of bugs and mosquitoes, mix Tulsi juice with an insecticide or with kerosene and use the mixture as a spray.

* If your cot is infested with bed-bugs, place a few twigs of the wild variety of Tulsi on the cot. The bugs will quickly run away. Mosquitoes, too, will not approach the cot. Even moles and snakes cannot bear the smell of the Tulsi twigs, and will keep away from the cot.

* The poison in a mosquito sting is destroyed by the application of Tulsi juice.

* In case of a sting or a bite of any poisonous insect or animal, rub the location of the sting or bite immediately with a few crushed Tulsi leaves. This will ensure a reduction in the severity of the effect of the poison.

* To counter the effects of the poison of a maniari, a very poisonous reptile, drink 10 grammes of Tulsi juice or chew some Tulsi leaves. If chewing is not possible because of a locked jaw under the effects of the poison, the juice can be dropped into the nostrils and rubbed on the crown of the head, the palms and the soles of the feet.

* If poison of any sort has been imbibed, the victim should go on drinking as much Tulsi juice as possible. This will ameliorate the effects of the poison.

7. TULSI : A REMEDY FOR ALL FEVERS

Malaria (Autumn Fever) : * Tulsi juice is highly beneficial in cases of malarial fevers. An incipient attack of malaria can be aborted by taking two or four leaves of the plant crushed with black pepper, or, if suffering from a cold as well, by drinking a decoction of the mixture.

* A decoction of Tulsi, black pepper and jaggery should be drunk while it is hot, after adding some lemon juice. After the drink one should lie down and cover oneself with a warm blanket. This procedure should be repeated every two or three hours. This treatment will cure malaria.

* Grind 10 grammes of Tulsi leaves and 10 black pepper seeds to a very smooth paste, roll the paste into pea-sized pills, and dry them in the shade. Two of these pills should be taken with water at intervals of 3 hours.

* Pulverise 10 grammes of Tulsi leaves, 10 grammes of black pepper, 10 grammes of the leaves of the bitter gourd creeper, and 10 grammes of kadu twigs by pounding them in a mortar. Prepare pea-sized pills of this mixture and dry them in the shade. If two of these pills are taken with cold water

every evening, and two pills are taken a little while before the anticipated attack of fever, especially the kind of fever that is preceded by cold rigours, the attacks will decrease in intensity and will cease after a few days. If a healthy person takes one of these pills every morning, he will be protected from attacks of fever. These pills cannot be stored for more than two months without getting spoilt, and losing efficacy.

* Warm equal amounts of the juices of Tulsi leaves and tender twigs of neem with some black peppers, and drink it while it is warm.

* Seven Tulsi leaves, four black pepper seeds and one gramme of kariatu twigs should be mixed well and taken in three portions daily.

* 10 grammes of Tulsi juice and 1 gramme of powdered black pepper should be mixed with 4 grammes of honey. The mixture is to be licked from a suitable container or a spoon.

* A malaria patient should be given a decoction of Tulsi roots. This will induce profuse perspiration and bring the temperature down.

* Malaria can be cured by taking 10 grammes of Tulsi juice every morning, noon and evening.

* Alternatively, 10 grammes of Tulsi juice mixed with 5 grammes of ginger juice can be taken with equal success.

* Dry Tulsi leaves in the shade and bake them in a pan over a medium flame. Take 15 grammes of such leaves. Take one gramme each of cloves, cardamoms, cinnamon and yeshti madhu, and powder them together. Drop all these into 100 grammes of boiling water, and take it off the fire after two minutes. Allow the decoction to cool for 5 minutes and then strain it. Drink the decoction after adding sugar and milk to taste.

* 100 grammes of Tulsi leaves and 10 grammes each of nutmeg, small peepar seeds, and black pepper seeds are ground together, formed into pea-sized pills and dried in the

shade. One of these pills should be taken four times a day at intervals of three hours.

* Grind 60 grammes of Tulsi leaves, petals of *mandar* flowers, petals of *datura* flowers and 10 grammes of black pepper with some water. Roll the paste into pea-sized pills. If two of these pills are taken at intervals of one hour, before the anticipated attack of malaria, the attack will be prevented.

* Grind 10 grammes of Tulsi leaves, 40 grammes of gram *(kangani)* powder, 20 grammes of katlee leaves and 10 grammes of black pepper together, and prepare pea-sized pills. Take two of these pills with an interval of one hour between them before the anticipated attack of malaria. Ordinarily two of these pills should be taken every morning and evening, while malaria is prevalent in the surrounding area. This will protect you from malaria.

* Drinking a mixture of equal parts of Tulsi leaf juice, neem leaf juice and the juice of large *(kagadi)* lemons is sure to prove beneficial.

* An extract prepared by boiling 10 grammes of Tulsi leaves and 10 grammes of *amaltas* pulp in water is an effective cure for malaria (autumn fever).

* 60 grammes of Tulsi leaves and 10 grammes each of the bark of *datura* roots and the bark of *mandar* roots are ground in a mortar and rolled into pea-sized pills. If these pills are taken three to four times at intervals of one or two hours before the attack of fever, the fevers known as kampajwar and vatajwar, as well as other fevers, can be cured.

* The characteristic smell of Tulsi repels mosquitoes, the carriers of the malarial parasites. Thus the juice of Tulsi leaves smeared over the exposed areas of the body will afford protection against mosquitoes, and hence against malaria.

* Juices of Tulsi and ginger taken with honey stimulate appetite and help to cure colds, fever and pneumonia.

* The juice of Tulsi leaves to which pinch of powdered black pepper has been added should be drunk four times a day. This will be beneficial in pneumonia.

Influenza (phlegmatic fever) : * Crush 50 grammes of Tulsi leaves and 5 black pepper seeds, and boil them in 200 grammes of water, till the volume of the water is reduced to half. Drink 50 grammes of this extract every morning, noon and evening.

* Considerable benefit is obtained by taking 10 grammes of a mixture of equal parts of powdered Tulsi leaves, *ajwan* seeds and stone (dry) ginger with some honey three times a day.

* Soak 25 grammes of Tulsi leaves in 250 grammes of hot water. Mash the leaves and strain the extract. Take 100 grammes of the extract every morning, noon and evening.

* Boil 10 grammes of Tulsi leaves in 150 grammes of water, till 50 grammes of water remain. Strain, and add some rock salt. Drink while it is still warm.

* 10 grammes of the parts of a Tulsi plant such as leaves, inflorescences and seeds are soaked in half a cup of honey or *'mritasanjeevani'* (revivifying) wine for a week, and the liquid is then strained. Two teaspoonfuls of this liquid taken three times a day will cure influenza (the fever caused by excess of phlegmatic humour).

* Boil 10 grammes of Tulsi leaf juice with a cupful of water till half of the water is boiled away. Add white (refined) sugar. This drink is a remedy for influenza.

* A patient should be given a mixture of 20 grammes of Tulsi juice, 10 grammes of ginger juice and some honey.

* Boil five leaves of Tulsi, 5 black pepper seeds and 5 grammes of ginger in one cupful of water. Add sugar to taste, and drink while it is still hot. This mixture is to be drunk every morning and evening.

* **Miscellaneous (any kind of common fever) :** During an epidemic of cholera, burn incense daily in the house, and

drink only boiled water. Make more liberal use of lemons, onions, garlic, buttermilk and Tulsi in your daily diet.

* For fevers due to colds, take the juice of Tulsi leaves with honey.

* Grind 11 leaves of Tulsi, 9 black pepper seeds, 30 grammes of *ajwan* seeds and 50 grammes of stone ginger in a mortar, and shake well with water. Take a newly prepared dry clay cup or crucible, heat it strongly, and pour the above mixutre into it. Expose your body to the vapours emanating from the hot mixture. When its temperature comes down to a tolerable level, add a little rock salt to the mixture and drink it off. Fever of any type will subside in a very short while.

* Taking 10 grammes of the mixed juice of mint and Tulsi leaves sweetened with 5 grammes of crystal sugar is very beneficial in chronic fevers.

* Those who are subject to attacks of malarial fever preceded by cold rigours should drink the decoction prepared by boiling 5 grammes each of Tulsi leaves, mint leaves and ginger.

* Pulverise leaves of Tulsi and those of the dark drumstick tree to a fine powder. This powder taken with lukewarm water cures typhoid fever.

* In case of mild fever, a well-ground mixture of 5 grammes of Tulsi leaves, 10 black raisins, 10 grammes of black pepper and two grammes of mint leaves taken with powdered crystal sugar is beneficial.

* Daily ingestion of 10 grammes of Tulsi leaf juice is beneficial in typhoid fever and chronic fever.

* If a fever is accompanied by cough and difficulty in breathing, take 3 grammes of Tulsi juice and 3 grammes of ginger juice with a teaspoonful of honey. The fever will subside and phlegm will be removed, making breathing easier.

* If there is continuous fever without remission, a paste obtained by grinding two small peepar seeds and mixing Tulsi

juice and honey with it, should be taken. This paste is to be licked, not to be swallowed with water.

* Drinking the juice obtained by grinding Tulsi leaves and sunflower leaves together is beneficial in all types of fevers.

* In mild fever accompanying a cold, drinking a decoction of Tulsi leaves to which milk and sugar have been added is of great benefit. These days many knowledgeable persons recognise the superior benefits of such a decoction as compared to tea.

* A decoction of Tulsi leaves, turmeric and black pepper gives relief in colds and concomitant mild fever.

* Any type of fever will yield to regular treatment with a drink made by grinding together 7 leaves of Tulsi, one leaf of *harsingar*, 3 betel leaves and three black pepper seeds in 50 grammes of water.

* 10 grammes of powdered black pepper and 10 grammes of *peepar* seeds are added to Tulsi juice, subjected 6 times to the process of maturation known as *Bhavna*, and rolled into pea-sized pills. These pills cure every type of fever.

* Regular ingestion of 2 grammes of powdered black pepper in 10 grammes of Tulsi juice every morning ensures protection against all types of fevers.

* Prepare a tea-like beverage by boiling 6 grammes of dry Tulsi leaves and 10 grammes of ginger in some water. Add hot milk and sugar, and drink while it is tolerably hot.

* Mix equal quantities of the leaves of Tulsi, mango tree, *bili (bilwa)*, *laajwanti* (mimosa) and the smaller variety of *chitraphala*, dry them in the shade and powder them. Ten grammes of this mixture boiled with water yields a salubrious drink.

* Powder 10 grammes of dry Tulsi leaves, 1 gramme of cinnamon, 1 gramme of saffron and the seeds of 3 cardamoms together. Boil the powder with water, add milk and sugar, and drink while warm.

* Form a habit of taking 10 grammes of Tulsi juice ground with 1 gramme of black pepper and 5 grammes of honey.

* Mix Tulsi leaf juice with aged jaggery and form into pills. These pills are to be taken one at a time.

* Grind together dry (stone) ginger and Tulsi leaves. Apply the resulting paste on the forehead, massaging lightly. Then lie down and cover the head. This will induce perspiration and bring the temperature down to normal.

* Drink a decoction of Tulsi leaves, black pepper and flowers of *jalakumbhi*.

* Licking a paste formed by mixing 5 grammes of powdered *peepar* with juices of 15 grammes of Tulsi, 15 grammes of tender neem shoots and 15 grammes of *guruch* leaves along with some honey is of benefit in chronic fever.

* Drink 10 grammes of Tulsi juice with 5 grammes of sugar.

* Grind together 10 grammes of Tulsi leaves, 5 grammes of black pepper and 10 grammes of tender shoots of *karanjlata*. Roll into pills. Chronic fever is cured by regular treatment with these pills.

* Take 10 grammes of Tulsi seeds, 10 grammes of peepar seeds and 10 grammes of the kernels of *karanjlata* seeds. Grind to a fine paste and prepare pea-sized pills. These pills constitute an effective remedy for fevers associated with abnormalities of semen.

* Drinking about half an ounce (12 grammes) of the extract of Tulsi roots eliminates mild fevers.

* A suspension obtained by crushing 6 leaves of Tulsi and 7 black pepper seeds with two teaspoonfuls of water is a cure for typhoid fever accompanied by loose motions.

* Licking a paste obtained by mixing 10 grammes of Tulsi juice, 5 grammes of powdered black pepper and a quarter teaspoonful of honey is a good remedy for typhoid.

* Another effective treatment for typhoid is the regular administration of pills rolled from a paste formed by grinding

10 Tulsi leaves, 10 black pepper seeds and a quarter teaspoonful of aged jaggery.

* Pound together equal amounts of leaves of Tulsi, *bili (bilwa)* and *peepar,* and add a cupful of water. Boil till the water is reduced to one-third, and strain the extract. 25 grammes of this extract taken at two-hour intervals will cure delirious fevers and other high fevers including typhoid.

* Take equal portions of dark Tulsi, Van Tulsi and mint. Crush them and press out the juice. This juice should be administered three times. If there is no favourable response, the treatment is to be continued for seven days. This is an efficacious remedy for mild fever.

* A decoction of Shyam Tulsi and dry (stone) ginger taken with sugar will abort an incipient attack of fever.

* Pound together 10 Tulsi leaves, 10 black pepper seeds, 10 grammes of the seeds of *khoobkala* (a variety of grass), 5 grammes of mint leaves and 10 grammes of coriander. Boil with a cupful of water in an earthen vessel. When a quarter of the water is left, strain the extract and add 10 grammes of crystal sugar. This extract is efficacious against colds and concomitant fever.

* In common colds and accompanying fevers, a tea-like decoction of Tulsi leaves is very effective. Take a few leaves of Shyam Tulsi, add some sugar and boil well in a cupful of water. Strain, and let the patient drink it with or without cow's milk, as preferred. This treatment continued over a few days will bring the temperature down to normal. The dosage for children would be about one-eighth of that for adults.

* Boil 10 grammes of Tulsi leaves in 250 grammes of water till half the water has been boiled away. Strain the extract. This extract is an effective remedy for common fevers.

* Pulverise 5 grammes of dry Tulsi leaves, two small cardamoms, 10 grammes of cinnamon and some saffron. Drop the powder into a cupful of boiling water and keep it covered

for 5 to 7 minutes. Add milk and sugar according to taste. This drink is not only delicious, but also a good remedy for fevers.

* Boil 5 grammes of dry Tulsi leaves, 2 grammes of ginger and 2 grammes of black pepper with water. Add milk and sugar. This drink is a remedy for fevers and chest pains caused by bound muscles.

* Administration of Tulsi juice, honey and *makardhwaj* in amounts suited to the condition of the patient cures the condition described as *'sheetang'*, characterised by slowing down of the pulse.

* Grind together 100 grammes of Tulsi leaves and 10*grammes each of black pepper, small *peepar* seeds and nutmeg in a mortar, roll into pea-sized pills, and dry them in the shade. These pills, taken one at a time with warm water 3 to 4 times a day, will induce perspiration, and the fever will subside. Children should be given a quarter of a pill of half a pill according to age. If the pills prove too 'hot', the dosage should be reduced.

* An extract of one or two pieces of *mulethi,* two black pepper seeds, a clove or two, sugar and the dark variety of Tulsi is easy to prepare, and very salubrious in effect. Treatment with this extract for seven days will cure both cough and fever.

* Monsoon, autumn and spring are seasons during which fevers and respiratory disorders are more prevalent. Chewing 20-25 Tulsi leaves every day during these seasons will afford protection against these disorders.

* Application of the juice of the leaves of Van Tulsi on all nails of the hands and the feet is effective against the lowering of the pulse rate *(sheetang)* caused by certain fevers such as typhoid.

* Mild fevers should be treated by administering the juices of Shyam Tulsi, Van Tulsi and mint for three to seven days.

* Nearly all types of fevers subside on treatment with Tulsi juice mixed with other suitable medicines such as *jwarankusha rasa, swachchhanda bhairava rasa, hinguleshwara rasa, agnikumara rasa* and the red variety of *mrityunjaya rasa,* the particular combination being selected according to the condition of the patient.

8. DISEASES OF WOMEN

The Tulsi plant has been ascribed feminity, and has been named accordingly. The scriptures regard it as dear to Lord Vishnu. It is therefore of special value in the treatment of diseases of women, and in promoting their health.

* Tying Tulsi roots to the waist is beneficial to women, especially when they are pregnant. The labour pains are less severe and delivery is easier.

* Continued excessive bleeding can be gradually reduced and ultimately stopped by regular treatment with Tulsi.

* Two grammes of each of these ingredients are taken and ground together : dry (stone) ginger, gum from the bark of a neem tree, *ajwan* seeds, *tamal patra,* and equal amounts of the 5 parts of the Tulsi plant. The powder so prepared is boiled in 100 grammes of water till one-fourth of the water remains. The extract is cooled and strained. Such extract should be taken regularly.

* If half a glass of water boiled with Tulsi leaves is taken for each of the three days starting from the day of menstruation, the probability of conception is greatly reduced. This method of contraception is especially useful as it does not harm the genital organs. On the contrary they are rendered healthier and more potent.

* In one of the ancient works on therapeutics, a method of curing infertility in women has been described thus :

"If the issues of any woman consistently fail to survive, massaging her limbs regularly and long-lived male child. If the same treatment is given to an infertile woman, she too becomes the mother of a beautiful male child within a year."

* If Tulsi is worshipped with sincerity and faith, and used according to the prescribed rituals, all physical and mental disorders are cured and the reproductive organs become capable of conception. In such a case, the boiled extract of leaves as well as powdered seeds and syrup are also useful. The extract should be taken for some days to purify the tissues and organs, and then the preparations of the seeds should be taken to strengthen the uterus. This will certainly increase the probability of achieving motherhood.

* Itching of the skin over the abdomen and the breasts of a pregnant woman is relieved by the application of the paste of Van Tulsi.

* If the uterus has been displaced, it can be restored to its proper position by sprinkling a finely powdered mixture of Tulsi and mango ginger on the genitalia. Crack-like stretch-marks are formed in the skin over the abdomen during pregnancy as the abdomen gets enlarged. In some cases this causes itching. A poultice of crushed Tulsi leaves gives complete relief in such cases.

* Cumin seeds ground in Tulsi juice and mixed with fresh milk of a cow have a beneficial effect in leucorrhoea, and they also improve the general health of the woman.

* If the menstrual flow is excessive, causing dizziness, Tulsi juice mixed with honey will give quick relief.

* Application of medicated oil prepared by boiling 125 grammes of Van Tulsi leaves in 500 grammes of seasame oil previously subjected to the process of *'moorchhana'*, relieves the pains associated with confinement.

* Tulsi seeds soaked overnight for twelve hours in water, crushed well in the morning and administered with sugar relieve the pains consequent upon delivery.

* Breast milk will improve in quality if the woman is given a mixture of 20 grammes of Tulsi juice, 20 grammes of the juice of maize leaves, 10 grammes of the juice–or extract–of *asgandh (ashwagandha)*, and 10 grammes of honey, for seven days following delivery.

* Leucorrhoea can be completely cured by treatment with 20 grammes of Tulsi juice with rice water, meanwhile restricting the diet to rice and milk, or rice and ghee for the duration of the treatment.

* Regular use of powdered roots of Tulsi enfolded in betel leaves stops the bleeding of the internal lining of the stomach.

* The adhesive property of Tulsi seeds makes them specially effective in diseases of the reproductive system of a woman. The seeds are helpful in amenorrhoea. Treatment with the seeds ground and suspended in water for three days beginning from the first day of the menstrual flow will help the woman to conceive, as this treatment purifies the uterus. If this treatment is given to any infertile woman for a year, she is sure to conceive.

* If the uterus is diseased or weak, so that every conception ends in miscarriage, regular treatment with Tulsi will make the uterus healthy and strong, and the woman will become the mother of a beautiful and healthy baby.

* 5 parts of the Tulsi plant, saffron, *gangeran*, the lighter coloured variety of grass known as *'dhro'* (gnodon), *putrakanda* and *shatavary* are ground together. This powder is mixed with milk collected directly from the teats of a cow that has a calf, and sugar is added. This preparation is given to the woman every day for ten days from the day of menstruation. This will ensure conception.

* One gramme of each of the following ingredients is taken : Tulsi seeds, *naagkesar, ashwagandha,* and *palash peepal.* These are then ground to a powder that is fine enough to pass through cloth. To this powder are added 10 grammes of cow's milk and some sugar. Administration of this preparation will restore regularity of menstruation within two months, even in the case of a woman who has stopped menstruating for some reason.

* 125 grammes of each of the following ingredients are taken and ground to a fine powder : Tulsi seeds, black seasame seeds, tender shoots of the cotton plant and tender shoots of bamboo plants. 220 grammes of aged jaggery are mixed with the powder and pea-sized pills are prepared. These pills taken one at a time with warm water every morning and evening will also restore regularity of periods, even in cases of women with amenorrhoea.

* Drinking Tulsi juice will lessen the severity of labour pains.

9. DISEASES OF MEN

* Leaves of Tulsi, *hadiakarshan* and *amarvel,* and droppings of camels are crushed and boiled in cow's urine to form a thick paste. Application of this paste in a thick layer on the scrotum is beneficial in hydrocele.

* A drink prepared by soaking 10 grammes of Tulsi seeds overnight in one cup of water, mashing them well in the liquid and adding sugar will relieve dysuria.

* 10 grammes of Tulsi juice taken with 5 grammes of water and cow's milk relieves dysuria and a burning sensation in the urinary passage.

* Dysuria can also be relieved by drinking a mixture of 10 grammes of Tulsi juice and 10 grammes of lemon juice.

* Chewing a few leaves of Tulsi daily for a few days is also beneficial in dysuria.

* In case of difficulty in or stoppage of urination, drinking Tulsi juice with double its quantity of grape juice, sugarcane juice or coconut milk will induce profuse urination.

Nocturnal Emissions : * Soak 10 grammes of Tulsi seeds overnight in water in an earthen pot. Grind them well in the morning with 15 almond kernels and 16 small cardamoms. Add sugar as required and drink the mixture. This will prevent nocturnal emissions.

* Small pieces of Tulsi roots chewed with betel leaves will also prevent nocturnal emissions.

* Regular ingestion of an extract of Tulsi leaves, cardamoms and 10 grammes of *sudhamooli* prepared by boiling them with water is beneficial in the prevention of nocturnal emissions. The drink is nutritious too.

* **Thinness of Seminal Fluid (Inadequacy of sperm-count) :** Powder 50 grammes of Tulsi seeds and 60 grammes of sugar together. Take 5 grammes of this powder with cow's milk every day.

* Take 50 grammes of Tulsi leaves, 40 grammes of *musli,* 40 grammes of the pods of *poshi,* 30 grammes of *kavach* seeds, 50 grammes of *gokhru* (small caltrops) and 60 grammes of sugar. Grind all these together to a powder fine enough to pass through cloth. Take 10 grammes of this powder with cow's milk every day.

* Take 5 grammes each of Tulsi seeds, *sudhamooli,* small cardamom seeds, *musli* and white *gokhru,* and powder them. Take 5 grammes of this powder and 5 grammes of sugar with milk every morning and evening.

Premature Ejaculation : * Cut Tulsi roots into thin slices. These slices taken with betel leaves increase the power of retention.

* 5 grammes of powdered Tulsi leaves taken with betel leaves are also beneficial.

* Two grammes of a mixture obtained by crushing Tulsi roots and *surti kand* (elephant yam) together, taken with betel leaves will also prove beneficial.

* Take 50 grammes of Tulsi seeds, 40 grammes of *musli*, and 60 grammes of crystal sugar, and powder them together. 10 grammes of this mixture taken with cow's milk every day will improve the quality of the seminal fluid.

* Sujak is a urinary disease related to chancroid. This disease is treated in the following manner : 5 grammes each of Tulsi seeds, seeds of small cardamoms and nitre are powdered together. 5 grammes of this powder are swallowed, followed by a drink of milk diluted with double its quantity of water. This lassi should be drunk in as large an amount as possible. It will prove highly beneficial. Of course, no sugar or any other substance should be added to it.

* Prepare a smooth paste by grinding Tulsi seeds with a little water. Boil the paste with twice its amount of neem oil. Let the mixture boil till the paste is blackened by the heat. Let the oil cool, separate it from the charred particles, and apply the oil on the sores caused by syphilis. This oil is highly beneficial in the treatment of other sores and wounds too.

* If there is pain and a burning sensation in the urinary passage while passing urine, prepare a mixture of 125 grammes of milk, 125 grammes of water, and 20 to 30 grammes of Tulsi leaf juice, and drink it up.

* Tulsi seeds yield a very slicky paste. They are useful in disorders of the urinary tract. Tulsi roots are reputed to greatly augment the powers of retention. They exhibit adhesive properties when ground, and their paste becomes very sticky in a short time. That is why they are generally taken as a suspension in water or after mixing with things like jaggery.

DISEASES OF MEN

* In case of thinness of the seminal fluid, make a practice of taking 15 grammes of Tulsi seeds with 30 grammes of aged sugar syrup every morning and evening.

* Soak 5 grammes of Tulsi seeds overnight in 125 grammes of water. In the morning, mash them thoroughly and drink the suspension. Regular and continued use of this preparation will prove of benefit in gonorrhoea, thinness of seminal fluid, dysuria and allied diseases.

* Mix Tulsi seeds and jaggery. Roll into pea-sized pills. If one of these pills is taken every morning and evening with cow's milk for four months, there will be an increase in the rate of formation of semen, the blood vessels will be strengthened, digestion will improve and impotence will be cured. However hopeless the condition of the man may have become, his sexual potency will be restored completely.

* Tulsi seeds ground with cumin seeds and sugar, taken with milk, are efficacious in the treatment of pains caused by stones in the bladder, burning sensation while passing urine and inflammation in the perineal region.

* Crushed Tulsi seeds taken with honey will cure all abnormalities of the genital system, including nocturnal emissions, gonorrhoea, etc.

* Regular use of Tulsi seeds eliminates pain accompanying urination.

* Powdered Shyam Tulsi mixed with lemon juice, if taken regularly, cures all abnormalities of the urinary system.

* Soak 10 grammes of Tulsi root powder in a cupful of water in the evening. Grind it well in the morning, mix well and strain the suspension. Drinking this extract daily will cure gonorrhoea.

* Gonorrhoea can also be cured by taking 40 grammes of powdered Tulsi seeds and 12 grammes of aged jaggery with milk collected straight from the teats of a cow. This will also

improve the quality of the seminal fluid. The treatment should be continued for 40 days.

* A mixture of equal parts of the powder of Tulsi leaves dried in the shade, powdered *methi* seeds and powdered *ashwagandha*, taken with cow's milk is also an effective remedy for gonorrhoea. It also improves the quality of the seminal fluid.

* Nocturnal emissions can be prevented by taking equal amounts of powdered Tulsi leaves, *sheetalchini* (cubebs) powder and camphor with cold water at the time of going to bed.

* Take 100 grammes of Tulsi leaves, 20 grammes each of *chopchini, taseemkhana, peeparimool, naagkesar* and *akkalgaro* (palatory root). Grind each of these separately to a fine powder, and soak each one in aged honey, using in all 200 grammes of honey. Keep aside for 24 hours. Prepare a thick syrup of 500 grammes of white (refined) sugar. Let it cool. Then stir the soaked ingredients along with the honey into the syrup. Now grind 100 grammes each of saffron, seeds of small cardamoms and *javantri* (mace) to a fine powder, add these powders also to the syrup, stir well and store in a glass jar. 10 to 20 grammes of this preparation are to be taken regularly with cow's milk sweetened with sugar, the amount being adjusted according to the state of your health. This proves efficacious in curing deterioration in the quality of the seminal fluid, loss of it through urine, and other allied disorders. Celibacy should be observed and diet should be restricted to salubrious items of food during the treatment.

* Regular ingestion of seeds of Van Tulsi soaked in water and mixed with crystal sugar powder is a good remedy for dysuria. The same treatment continued for a sufficiently long period will cure all other diseases of the urino-genital system.

* Debility can be successfully treated by regular administration of the five parts of the Tulsi plant (leaves, seeds, etc.) powdered together with crystal sugar.

10. DISEASES OF CHILDREN

* Tulsi constitutes very mild and harmless medication for the treatment of children's diseases. Many of children's disorders such as fevers, coughs, regurgitation of milk, difficulty in breathing, etc., yield very promptly to treatment with Tulsi.

* Tulsi juice should be warmed before it is given to children. Where Tulsi seeds are recommended, 2 to 5 grammes will suffice in most cases where children are concerned. This amount can be given three to four times a day. Even healthy children will be benefited by the regular administration of Tulsi juice, as this will help them to maintain their health and prevent sickness.

* In case of fever caused by a cold, Tulsi juice should be smeared on the chest and forehead. The child should be made to inhale the vapours emanating from the juice, and should also be given a teaspoonful of the juice with half a teaspoonful of honey.

* If the child brings up worms with its vomit, or excretes worms with faeces, give it a little powdered *vavding, kakcha* or *himej* with 10 grammes of Tulsi juice two or three times a day.

* In case of dry cough, the child should be given tender shoots of Tulsi and ginger crushed together and mixed with honey. The paste is to be licked, not to be swallowed with water.

* If a baby is given Tulsi juice regularly before teething, it will cut its teeth easily without any of the usual teething troubles.

* Prompt administration of Tulsi juice in the initial stages of colds, fevers, accumulation of phlegm, vomiting or diarrhoea will be of great benefit.

* 5 grammes of Tulsi inflorescences, 5 grammes of *vaj peepar* (sweet flag) and 20 grammes of crystal sugar are boiled in 500 grammes of water until half of the water is boiled away,

and the extract is filtered. One teaspoonful of this extract administered four or five times a day will cure dry cough.

* If an infant develops a cough, it will be benefited by the administration of a mixture of five grammes of Tulsi leaves, five grammes of *kakdashingi* and five grammes of *ativish* buds crushed together, made into a paste with honey and the mother's milk.

* Cough can also be cured by letting the child lick Tulsi juice mixed with *jethi madh (yashti madhu) juice*.

* A mixture of Tulsi leaf juice and *kasondara* leaf juice is also a good remedy for coughs.

* Boil 10 grammes of Tulsi leaves, 10 grammes of *methi* seeds and 5 grammes of *kadu* twigs in 50 grammes of water till only one-fourth of the water remains. Cool and strain. Administration of this extract is beneficial in fevers preceded by cold rigours, such as malaria.

* If the child has abdominal pains, a slightly warmed mixture of Tulsi and ginger juices will provide relief.

* 5 grammes each of Tulsi leaf juice, *ajawan* seeds and turmeric are ground to a very fine paste in mortar. Twenty-five grammes of honey are added, mixed well, and the mixture stored in a glass container. Thirty to sixty drops of this mixture administered two to three times a day to a child suffering from a cold or cough will prove greatly beneficial.

* Take ten grammes of each of the following ingredients : Tulsi leaves, tender shoots of the *babul* tree, and *ajwan* seeds. Grind them to a paste. Five grammes of this paste are to be boiled with 50 grammes of water till only one-fourth of water remains. The extract is strained and sweetened with some sugar. Administration of this extract to a child having fever is sure to prove beneficial, no matter what type of fever it is.

* If the abdomen of a baby is distended due to the accumulation of gas, the condition can be relieved by giving it 5 to 10 grammes of Tulsi juice, the exact amount given depending on the age of the baby.

* In case of diarrhoea accompanying teething, powdered Tulsi leaves should be given to the child with pomegranate syrup.

* Letting the baby lick a mixture of Tulsi juice and honey will bring quick relief in cough and sore throat.

* If a cough is the result of excessive accumulation of phlegm, the juice of Shyama Tulsi mixed with honey will help. This mixture is of great value in the treatment of a child with a tendency to vomit frequently.

* In case a baby is suffering from colic, giving it a little powdered stone (dry) ginger with Tulsi leaf juice will afford relief.

* If a child has worms, a mixture composed of two grammes of *vavding* powder, half a gramme of asafoetida, two teaspoonfuls of Tulsi juice and half a spoonful of honey should be given to it twice a day, in the morning and evening. The mixture is to be licked, not to be swallowed with water.

* If an infant being fed on breast milk suffers from vomiting and retching, it should be given three drops of Tulsi juice mixed with honey to lick.

* If an infant is suffering from a cold or cough, brew tea with four to five Tulsi leaves, and give one or two teaspoonfuls of this tea to the child in the morning and evening. This treatment continued for two days will effect a cure.

* Massaging the gums with Tulsi leaf juice mixed with honey will help the baby cut its teeth easily, without the usual troubles associated with teething.

* Five to ten drops of Tulsi leaf juice given with water every day will strengthen the muscles and bones of the infant.

* Influenza and coughs can be cured by regular administration of 30 to 60 drops of a mixture of 15 grammes of Tulsi leaf juice, 15 grammes of honey, 5 grammes of ginger juice and 5 grammes of powdered *ajwan* seeds.

* Fevers and coughs can also be cured by giving the child 10 to 30 drops (according to its age) of a suspension of 2 grammes of black pepper powder in 15 grammes of Tulsi juice in which 5 grammes of crystal sugar have been dissolved.

* Heat 200 grammes of Tulsi leaf juice with 125 grammes of water. Let the liquid simmer for one hour on a low flame. Prepare a thick syrup of 500 grammes of sugar, and stir the mixture into the syrup. Administration of 3 to 5 grammes of this preparation to a child cures fever, cough and shortness of breath.

* If there is a whistling sound heard from the lungs because of the accumulation of phlegm due to exposure to cold winds, the child should be given milk in which Tulsi leaves have been boiled, and should be made to lie down with warm covering over its body. This procedure is sure to relieve the condition.

* If a child suffering from fever is given two to three grammes of powdered *peepar* and five grammes of crystal sugar in 10 grammes of Tulsi juice, the fever will subside.

* Two grammes of powdered Tulsi seeds in breast milk or in cow's milk will cure a baby of diarrhoea.

* Take equal amounts of these ingredients : Tulsi seeds, *naagar moth, atees, kakadashingi,* stamens of the flowers of the smaller variety of *kateri (chitraphala), vavding,* roasted cumin seeds, the smaller variety of *peepar,* bamboo manna *(vansh lochan)* and saffron. Grind them together to a paste and form into small pills of the size of green grams. If these pills are given to a child every night for four or five days, a large variety of diseases can be cured, including fever, diarrhoea, difficulty in breathing, dyspnea, cough, vomiting, dacryocystitis, excessive movement of the ribs due to strain in breathing, etc.

* Warmed Tulsi juice will get rid of worms in the stomach of a child.

* The extract of Tulsi leaves cures a child of *'vistambh'*, or thrombosis.

* The extract of Tulsi roots sweetened with sugar will relieve constipation and distension of the stomach, ensuring a satisfactory bowel movement.

* Flatulence caused by indigestion can be relieved by a warm mixture of equal parts of Tulsi juice and betel leaf juice.

* Ten grammes of Tulsi leaves and ten grammes of peepar are ground together to a paste and rolled into small pills of the size of green grams. Three or four of these pills given to a child every day will cure coughs, including whooping cough.

* Take 5 grammes of each of these ingredients : Tulsi inflorescences, *vachh*, small *peepar*, and *mulethi*. Add 25 grammes of sugar. Add 250 grammes of water and boil till only 100 grammes of water are left. Cool and strain. Administration of 5 grammes of this extract five to six times during the day and also during the night will cure the child of dry hollow cough.

* An extract of Tulsi leaves and inflorescences given with jaggery to a child will afford relief in difficulty in breathing.

* Difficulty in breathing can also be relieved by giving 3 to 5 grammes of Tulsi juice to the child according to its age.

* Powdered Tulsi seeds given to a child with milk will relieve vomiting.

* Powdered bark of Tulsi roots given with honey helps an obese child to shed some of the fat.

* Extract of Tulsi is an effective remedy for liver disorders of children.

* A few drops of warmed Tulsi juice in the ears will relieve earache.

* Juices of Tulsi and ginger warmed together, and given with honey when cold to a child keeps the child healthy, and frees it from the threat of disorders like retention of urine and

stool, constipation, indigestion, vomiting, hiccups, shortness of breath, cough, fever, cold, etc.

* Tulsi juice is mixed with an equal quantity of *'choornodak'* (prepared by shaking lumps of quicklime with water, allowing the suspension to settle, and decanting the clear upper liquid, which is 'choornodak', lime water), and sugar or syrup is added. 5 to 60 drops of this mixture should be regularly given to the child, according to its age. This will cure the child of almost all diseases, and keep it healthy.

* All diseases of children yield to treatment with Tulsi leaf powder mixed with powdered sweet *vachh* and honey. The dosage should be adjusted in accordance with the age of the child.

11. VATA DISORDERS, RHEUMATISM AND PAINFUL JOINTS

* Tulsi possesses the property of curing disorders caused by variations in the proportion of the vata humour in the body. If there are neuralgic pains due to excessive formation of vata, Tulsi decoction will prove beneficial. In case of pain in the joints Tulsi leaf juice would be more appropriate.

* The roots, leaves, inflorescences, twigs and seeds of a plant constitute what is collectively known as its 'panchang', its five parts. The 'panchang' of Tulsi, with each of its parts having its own specific curative properties, is of importance in therapeutics. Take equal amounts of each of these five parts of the Tulsi plant. Grind them together, and pass through a fine mesh. Ten grammes of this mixture mixed with an equal amount of aged jaggery, and taken with goat's milk every morning and evening will relieve pain in the joints.

* Tulsi juice mixed with powdered black pepper and pure ghee is an effective remedy for inflammation caused by vata.

VATA DISORDERS, RHEUMATISM AND PAINFUL JOINTS

* Repeated administration of 5 grammes of a mixture of the juices of Shyama Tulsi, garlic and onions, and smearing the mixed juices all over the body is beneficial in tetanus as well as spasms due to other causes.

* A fine powder is prepared by grinding 5 grammes of Shyama Tulsi leaves, 3 grammes of meudi (sindhuar) leaves, 5 grammes of *bhangra*, and 3 grammes of the bark of *varuna* according to specified procedure. The powder is mixed with five grammes of honey. This paste is a cure for all conditions due to excessive vata, such as pains, inflammations, etc.

* Taking 5 grammes each of Tulsi juice and ginger juice regularly for a few days will also cure disorders caused by vata.

* Tulsi juice to which powdered black pepper and honey have been added is also effective in curing such disorders.

* Another effective treatment for this kind of disorders is an extract prepared by boiling Tulsi leaves and the roots of the castor plant. The extract is to be allowed to cool, and taken with honey.

* Pains in the flanks and other pains caused by vata can be relieved by applying the warmed paste prepared by grinding Tulsi juice, ginger juice and the powdered roots of *pushkar* together.

* The use of a decoction of Tulsi leaves for bathing and for the fomentation of the joints is effective in the treatment of rheumatism.

* Fomentation with a decoction of Tulsi leaves, or steam fomentation with the decoction of the five parts (panchang) of the Tulsi plant will cure vata disorders caused by mercury poisoning.

* Pain in the joints can be relieved by applying a poultice of a paste of Tulsi leaves, castor leaves and saindhav (rock salt).

* Tulsi seed powder is a good remedy for muscular pain.

* Regular treatment with Tulsi juice over a period of a few years will eliminate all abnormalities of blood caused by excess of vata.

* Exposure to the smoke generated by Drudrih Tulsi leaves dropped on glowing charcoal proves beneficial in all cases of abnormalities of blood due to vata, including rheumatism and oedema of the hands and feet.

* Rheumatoid arthritis can be cured by fomentation with steam from water boiled with Drudrih Tulsi leaves, and drinking the decoction when it cools to bearable temperatures.

* Fomentation with steam from the boiling decoction of the five parts (panchang) of the Van Tulsi plant is beneficial in all paralytic conditions such as paralysis of the torso, facial paralysis, paralysis caused by mercury poisoning and paralysis caused by abnormal functioning of the glands of the body due to excess of vata.

* Take 100 grammes of each of the following ingredients, and grind them together in cow's urine :

Panchang of Tulsi, panchang of neem, panchang of kateli (a variety of the cotton plant), leaves of white sindhuar, leaves of amar vel and black makay (maize). Cook 125 grammes of the paste in seasame oil over a low flame. When all the moisture is expelled, cool and strain the oil. Use this oil to massage the joints and other parts affected by rheumatism.

* The following measures are beneficial in the treatment of paraplegia :

(1) Wash the affected parts with an extract of the panchang of the Tulsi plant.

(2) Apply a paste of crushed Tulsi seeds over the affected parts.

(3) Prepare an extract of the leaves, roots and flowers of the following five plants :

Tulsi, neem, bili (bilwa), indrajav and ganiari. Massage the affected parts with the extract while it is still fairly hot. Drink suitable quantities of the extract at intervals.

12. COLDS, COUGHS AND OTHER RESPIRATORY DISEASES

Some of the causes of the common cold are exposure to cold winds or bathing in cold water while perspiring with exertion or heat, drinking cold water immediately after violent physical activity, exposure to cold surroundings, sleeping in the open where the formation of dew can cause a sudden fall in temperature, etc. Blockage or dripping of the nose, a bad taste in the mouth, loss of the sensation of smell, headache, etc. are the chief symptoms of the condition.

One must seek the protection of Tulsi as soon as the symptoms of a cold such as dripping of the nose or secretion of phlegm are noticed. This will keep the disorder under check and prevent it from worsening, because Tulsi has a wonderfully salubrious action on the nasal passages and the respiratory system.

* Whether a cold is the result of exposure or an allergic reaction, Tulsi will help to get rid of it and its concomitant fever in a few days. For this purpose, a hot decoction of dry ginger, black pepper, Tulsi and jaggery should be drunk every two or three hours.

* Tulsi is the best remedy for dry cough as well as ordinary cough with secretion of phlegm.

* Four or five roasted cloves chewed with Tulsi leaves are beneficial in all types of coughs.

* If you have a dry cough or your voice has become hoarse due to a sore throat, grind equal amounts of Tulsi leaves, poppy seeds and *jethi madh (yashti madhu)* together and take the mixture with an equal quantity of sugar in warm water.

* Chest pains and coughs are relieved by drinking Tulsi juice with crystal sugar.

* Tea brewed with Tulsi leaves is a good remedy for fevers, colds and muscular pains.

* If you develop a cold, observe a complete fast for one day and take only light food the next day. Meanwhile take two teaspoonfuls of Tulsi juice and two teaspoonfuls of ginger juice with honey every morning and evening.

* Licking a paste formed by mixing camphor and honey with Tulsi juice, without added water, will relieve congestion in the chest due to thickened phlegm.

* If suffering from chronic cold, drink a hot decoction of cloves, cinnamon, dry ginger, black pepper, *peepar,* Tulsi, cardamom, *kakdashingi,* fern *(hansraaj), bankoosha* and *tamal patra* every morning and evening.

* Crush seven Tulsi leaves and five black pepper seeds to a fine paste and roll into pills. Take one pill every morning, noon and evening with water. Coughs and colds will be eradicated completely within a week.

* Ingestion of 5 grammes of Tulsi leaf juice mixed well with two powdered black pepper seeds and 5 grammes of sugar will relieve stiffening of the chest muscles and will also cure chronic fever.

* Drinking a decoction of ten grammes of Tulsi leaves to which appropriate quantities of sugar and cow's milk have been added, will prevent coughs and breathing difficulties caused by congestion of the chest. If the decoction is taken regularly, it will cure long-standing complaints of this nature.

* Take 10 grammes of each of the following ingredients :

Tulsi inflorescences, *vachh, peepar* and *mulethi.* Add 5 grammes of sugar and 5 grammes of large raisins. Add 500 grammes of water and boil till only 125 grammes of water are left. Drinking this extract in proper quantities as needed will cure dry cough. This extract can be given even to infants.

* Regular ingestion of an extract prepared by boiling equal quantities of Tulsi leaves, dry ginger, the smaller variety of *chitraphala, brahmadandi* and *kalthee* in water in accordance with the prescribed procedure will cure coughs and asthma.

COLDS, COUGHS AND OTHER RESPIRATORY DISEASES

* If an extract of equal quantities of Tulsi, *guruchi (amrita)*, dry ginger, the smaller variety of *chitraphala* and *vabhanethi* is taken regularly, it will cure hiccups and asthma.

* Taking 10 grammes of Tulsi juice with 5 grammes of honey will also cure hiccups and asthma.

* Hiccups and asthma can also be cured by taking an extract of equal quantities of Tulsi leaves and inflorescences with aged jaggery.

* A mixture of equal quantities of the juices of the bark of Van Tulsi and *aradoosi (bansa)* is an effective remedy for coughs.

* Smoking a bidi rolled from Tulsi leaves cures a freshly contracted cold.

* Regular ingestion of powdered Krishna Tulsi seeds cures disorders caused by abnormal amounts of the phlegmatic humour.

* Taking equal quantities of powdered Tulsi leaves, powdered black pepper and *saindhav* rock salt, and rubbing the juice of Tulsi leaves all over the body will cure the colds.

* Licking 10 grammes of the juice of Barbari Tulsi leaves mixed with jaggery, powdered seeds of two cardamoms and some honey arrests the excessive secretion of phlegm.

* For relief in an attack of asthma, prepare a decoction by boiling 5 grammes of Tulsi inflorescences and 10 grammes of dry ginger in water, allow it to cool, mix some honey with it, and drink it. Take such a decoction twice or thrice as necessary.

* If there is pain in the ribs due to cold, apply a paste obtained by mixing 5 grammes of powdered pusker seeds with 5 grammes of Tulsi juice.

* If the cold has been caused by a drenching in the rain or excessive humidity in the air, drinking a decoction of Tulsi, dry ginger, cloves, cinnamon and black pepper three or four times in a day will effect a cure.

* An extract of 10 grammes of Tulsi leaves will cure coughs, chest pains, colds, and allied disorders.

* A mixture of 15 grammes of Tulsi juice, 25 grammes of pure honey and 5 grammes of ginger juice, taken in doses of 25 to 60 drops will cure coughs and fevers.

* A mixture of equal quantities of powdered Tulsi seeds and sugar is a good remedy for dry coughs and wheezing sounds in the chest.

* Boil 100 grammes each of Tulsi leaves, the *panchang* (five parts) of *bhoringani (kateri)*, dry ginger, *ardoosi (bansa)* or ginger. Add honey when the decoction has cooled. This decoction is a remedy for coughs.

* If suffering from a headache, whether caused by a cold, excess of *vata* or migraine, take five grammes of powdered Tulsi leaves with honey. The paste is to be licked (not to be swallowed with water). The paste is to be taken every morning and evening. Other measures that can be taken with advantage are applying a paste of crushed Tulsi leaves to the forehead and instilling two drops of the juice of Tulsi leaves into each of the nostrils.

* A decoction of Tulsi leaves or an extract of the leaves with black pepper or *mulethi* is very beneficial in the treatment of colds. Chewing black pepper seeds with Tulsi leaves every morning for forty days will cure chronic fevers and colds.

* Boil 5 grammes each of Tulsi leaves, wheat bran and *mulethi* in 200 grammes of water till half of the water has been boiled off, and strain the extract. This extract is beneficial in the treatment of colds, fevers and coughs.

* Licking a mixture of Tulsi juice and honey relieves soreness of the throat, colds, coughs, etc.

* Licking a paste obtained by crushing equal quantities of Tulsi inflorescences and ginger and mixing them with honey, three or four times a day relieves dry cough.

COLDS, COUGHS AND OTHER RESPIRATORY DISEASES

* Taking a paste obtained by crushing Tulsi leaves and four or five roasted cloves together will also prove beneficial in the treatment of coughs.

* If phlegm has been secreted in excessive quantities, drinking a decoction of 5 grammes each of Tulsi leaves, *naagar, moth (musta)* and dry ginger will rid the system of the excess phlegm.

* Oil with medicinal properties can be obtained from Tulsi leaves, black pepper, dry ginger, *peppar (piper longum), saindhav, dantimool,* the roots of the bitter gourd creeper, drumstick seeds, etc. Instilling a few drops of this oil into the nostrils from time to time is beneficial.

* Coughs are caused by exposure to cold air, drinking water immediately after the ingestion of fatty (oily) substances, drinking water while perspiring, etc. There are two kinds of coughs. In one, there is a feeling of irritation in the throat, but no expectoration of phlegm. This is dry cough. The other kind of cough is accompanied by expectoration of phlegm, as well as hoarseness of the voice, pain in the chest, headache, etc. Both kinds of coughs can be relieved by inhaling the vapours arising from Tulsi seeds being heated in a little ghee (clarified butter). Some warm milk must be taken after such inhalations.

* A paste formed by grinding together Tulsi seeds, onions and ginger and mixing with honey is beneficial in dry cough and infantile asthma. The paste is to be licked.

* Green Tulsi leaves grilled over an open fire taken with a little common salt are beneficial in coughs and pharyngitis.

* Regular ingestion of an extract of 10 grammes each of Tulsi leaves, *kulthee, brahmadandee,* dry ginger and the smaller variety of *chitraphala* is beneficial.

* 10 grammes of Tulsi leaves are dried in the shade and roasted in a pan over a low flame. These are powdered with 5 grammes each of *mulethi,* cloves, cinnamon and the seeds of small cardamoms. The resulting powder is dropped into

100 grammes of boiling water. After 5 minutes the decoction is taken off the fire, and milk and sugar are added. This extract constitutes a drink that cures not only coughs, but malaria, vomiting and persistent thirst also.

* Tulsi possesses the property of destroying the phlegmatic humour. It therefore exhibits the greatest efficacy in the treatment of disorders of the respiratory system. Tulsi is included in all Ayurvedic formulations used for the treatment of asthma. Charak too has emphasised the fact that Tulsi is an infallible remedy for respiratory diseases.

* One of the remedies for asthma is prepared as follows :

Five grammes each of the following ingredients are taken :

The *panchang* (five parts of the plant) of Tulsi, the yellow leaves of oak, *aradoosa (bansa) leaves, bhang* (cannabis) and cactus branch. These are ground together to a fine powder. A little *sambhar* rock salt is added. The mixture is placed in a small earthen pot. It is covered up completely with cloth and clay. Now the pot is heated for the duration of a *prahar* (about 3 hours) in a fire in which only the wood of wild forest trees is being burnt. The pot is then allowed to cool. It is then opened and the contents are ground well once again. The powder is then sieved and stored in a suitable container. Five grammes of this powder are to be taken three times a day with honey for the treatment of asthma.

* If phlegm has become too viscid and coughing cannot bring it up for expectoration, lick a paste formed by mixing the juices of Tulsi, onions and ginger with an equal quantity of pure honey. This will help the detachment of the phlegm which will then be easily expectorated.

* Boil 11 leaves of Tulsi, 2 or 3 black pepper seeds, a small piece of ginger and a pinch or *saindhav* rock salt in a cupful of water till only half a cup of water is left. Take the extract off the fire and strain it. Drinking this extract in three portions will cure colds and coughs.

TULSI-CLOCIMUM

The Regional Research Institute, Jammu has developed a new variety of Tulsi, which has been named 'clocimum' (the name being derived from 'clove' and 'ocimum', part of the Latin name for the Tulsi plant, Ocimum Sanctum).

The institute has developed this variety by the selective hybridization of about fifty different varieties of Tulsi, collected from various countries. It has taken the institute nearly two years to develop this new variety. It has been grown successfully in the grounds of the institute, and also in some private farms. From the scientific point of view, this achievement is described as revolutionary.

Clove oil is used in a large number of formulations. It is obtained from the flowers of a certain plant, which cannot be grown extensively in India. The oil has therefore to be imported, at a great cost.

The major constituent of clove oil is enginol, making up about eighty-five per cent of the oil. Clocimum, too, yields an oil that contains enginol to the extent of eighty-five per cent. But while enginol obtained from cloves costs nearly four hundred rupees per kilogramme, enginol from clocimum is expected to cost only half that amount.

According to the Research Institute, the development of clocimum will provide a cheaper alternative for imported clove oil. It will also constitute a cheaper source of enginol, which is used in innumerable important medicinal preparations.

13. BLISTERS, BOILS, WOUNDS AND SKIN DISEASES

Tulsi is endowed with purifying and antiseptic qualities to a relatively greater extent. It contains a volatile oil, the strong smell of which destroys many kinds of harmful micro-organisms. Tulsi has been mentioned in many passages in the chapter on 'Vish Chikitsa' in Charak's celebrated book. The antiseptic qualities of Tulsi have been described in detail in this chapter. Tulsi leaves are used in the treatment of the stings of wasps, scorpions, etc. The application of powdered Tulsi leaves on wounds hastens the process of healing. Washing wounds with a decoction of Tulsi leaves is also beneficial. The use of Tulsi in the treatment of ringworm, itching, dark patches on the skin, acne and other skin diseases proves beneficial. The efficacy of the remedies of skin diseases is greatly augmented if they are used in conjunction with Tulsi.

* Equal amounts of the five parts (panchang) of the Tulsi plant are dried and powdered together. An extract of this powder has a purifying action on the blood. Regular use of this extract therefore prevents skin diseases.

* Application of a paste formed by grinding Tulsi leaves with lemon juice is an effective treatment for ringworm.

* Continued ingestion of powdered Tulsi roots and leaves with hot water cures all skin diseases including serious diseases like leprosy.

* Soak Tulsi leaves and dried *anvla* fruits (Indian gooseberry) in water. If this water is used for washing the hair, the black colour of hair that has turned grey or white will be restored, and loss of hair will also be prevented.

* Application of crushed Tulsi and neem leaves is invariably beneficial in all skin diseases.

* Boil Tulsi leaves in oil of *sarasao (sarason)*. When the leaves have turned completely black, take the oil off the fire and strain it. This oil is beneficial in all skin diseases.

BLISTERS, BOILS, WOUNDS AND SKIN DISEASES

* If suffering from scabies, ringworm, eczema or pruritus, drink Tulsi juice and apply it on the affected parts. Use a decoction of Tulsi leaves for bathing.

* If a wound is festering because of infestation with micro-organisms, and blood is oozing out of it, wash the wound with Tulsi decoction which is just bearably hot, and apply a paste of crushed Tulsi leaves.

* Dry Tulsi leaves in the shade, add some alum, grind well and sieve through fine cloth. Store the powder in a clean dry glass bottle. This powder can be applied on any fresh cuts or wounds, and will promote quick healing.

* Application of Tulsi juice on boils is beneficial and gives relief.

* The use of Tulsi in the treatment of all kinds of cuts, wounds and ulcers is highly beneficial. Quick relief is obtained by the application of a paste obtained by rubbing the woody stem of Tulsi on a flat stone, like sandalwood. If foul odours are emanating from a wound because of infestation with various organisms, the wound should be washed with a hot decoction of Tulsi, and the powder of dried Tulsi leaves should then be applied.

* If eruptions or areas of localised swelling with decolorization are caused by *'sheetpitta'* (urticaria), apply Tulsi juice over the affected areas. This should be followed by daily application of crushed Tulsi leaves mixed with black clay.

* Application of Tulsi leaves ground in water from the river Ganga makes skin eruptions subside in a very short time.

* Application of a paste of Tulsi leaves and tender shoots of *peepar* (piper longum) on boils caused by infection resulting from the plucking of hair affords relief.

* Pain due to burns is alleviated by applying equal quantities of Tulsi juice and coconut oil mixed well. Blisters and wounds caused by the burn will also heal quickly.

* Healing of wounds is hastened by sprinkling finely powdered alum and dry Tulsi leaves on them.

* Boils in the armpits come to a head, burst and heal, on application of a warm poultice of Tulsi leaves, mustard seeds, jaggery and *googal (mukul)* ground together.

* Tulsi leaves and roots prove beneficial in the treatment of almost all skin diseases because of their powerful antiseptic properties. Grind 200 to 250 grammes of Tulsi leaves with water, and squeeze out the juice by pressing them. Boil 250 grammes of this liquid with 250 grammes of seasame seed oil. When all the water has been boiled off, strain the oil and store it in a glass bottle. Massage with this oil cures a large variety of skin diseases, including itching.

* If the procedure described above (massage with the medicated oil) is followed regularly, along with regular ingestion of powdered Tulsi roots and dry ginger with warm water every morning, even a terrible disease like leprosy can be cured. A renowned doctor has reported that a sanyasin had restored to complete health a leprosy patient whose disease had advanced to a stage when even his fingers had begun to be consumed. This cure was effected by the sanyasin by administering Tulsi juice to the patient continuously for a year without break.

* As Tulsi has a purifying action on the blood, it can be used to cure all diseases caused by abnormalities of the blood, such as blisters, boils, furuncles, eruptions, etc. Take 50 grammes of lemon juice in a copper vessel. Add 50 grammes of Tulsi juice, and the same quantity of the juice of black *kasondra*. Keep the vessel in sunlight. The juices will begin to lose water by evaporation. Expose the vessel to sunlight daily till all the water is lost and a dry residue is left. The residue will be almost black in colour. Application of this residue all over the face not only cures acne, black spots and other similar disorders, but also improves the appearance and beautifies the face. Treatment with this powder also cures white spots on the skin due to leucoderma.

* Ringworm can be cured by applying a paste formed by grinding Tulsi leaves and leaves of the lemon tree with curds.

* White spots on the face or any other area of the skin are commonly called 'spiders'. Apply the clay adhering to the roots of a Tulsi plant on the affected parts immediately on rising in the morning, even before cleaning your mouth. Improvement will be evident in a few days.

* Loss or greying of hair at an early age is the result of a kind of skin disease. Treatment consists of rubbing the skin of the head vigorously with Tulsi leaves and powdered *anvlas* (Indian gooseberry fruits). If this is done regularly every day, the roots of the hair become strengthened, hair begins to grow more profusely, and becomes black, smooth and soft.

* Dressing a wound with crushed Tulsi leaves assists healing. So does a paste of ground Tulsi seeds.

* Rubbing with Tulsi leaves over itching parts brings quick relief.

* Application of Tulsi leaves ground with red clay is an effective remedy for ringworm.

* Ringworm can also be cured by applying crushed Tulsi leaves. A mixture of Tulsi leaf juice, ghee prepared from cow's milk and lime, stirred well in a bronze vessel, applied twice a day, is also a cure for ringworm.

* A festering wound exuding pus and blood will stop oozing and begin to heal if a paste of ground Tulsi leaves is applied.

* Treatment of a wound with a powder consisting of equal parts of Tulsi and camphor destroys the micro-organisms infesting it.

(Advantage can be taken of the power of Tulsi to cure leprosy by planting large numbers of Tulsi plants, forming 'Tulsi Vans' in the grounds of all leprosy hospitals.)

* Micro-organisms infesting a wound can also be destroyed by filling the wound with the powder obtained by grinding dry twigs of Tulsi and betel leaves together.

* Leprosy patients are benefited by drinking the juice of Tulsi leaves to which white (refined) sugar has been added.

* Finely powdered Tulsi roots enfolded in betel leaves taken regularly will cure the kind of leprosy described as *'adhogami'*, i.e., spreading downwards.

* Itching can be soothed by taking Tulsi juice with powdered *majuphal,* and applying a mixture of Tulsi and lemon juice.

* The type of leprosy described as *'gajakarna'* leprosy can be successfully treated by applying a well-stirred homogenized mixture of ghee, lime, Tulsi juice and betel leaf juice.

* Twenty grammes of Tulsi leaves ground with one clove of garlic yield a paste the application of which cures ringworm.

* Rubbing Tulsi juice over the affected parts cures ringworm, eczema and other skin diseases.

* Rubbing clay adhering to Tulsi roots all over the body, taking a bath after a short interval of time, and wiping the body with a clean wet cloth cures all skin diseases. This procedure also protects people in good health from risk of skin diseases.

* Take 10 grammes each of Tulsi juice, pure mercury and pure opium in an iron container. Stir continuously for nine hours with a stick made from a branch of a neem tree. Add 10 grammes of pure borax and (an equal quantity of) Tulsi juice. Stir for 3 hours more. Add 25 grammes of the powders of each of these ingredients : mace *(jaypatri),* nutmeg, *akkalgaro* (palatory root), and *khurasani ajwan* seeds. Stir again with Tulsi juice for a further period of 3 hours. Add 250 grammes of powdered *vanshlochan* (bamboo manna) and 250 grammes of powdered *kher.* Stir for one *ghatika* (24 minutes). Roll the resulting paste into pea-sized pilis, dry the pills in the shade, and store them in a glass bottle. Taking two of these pills daily will cure syphilis, the *'galit's firangi'* type of leprosy, herpes, chancroid, etc. During the period of treatment with these pills, one should abstain from salt, pepper,

chillies, sour foods and jaggery. It is also necessary that the bowels should have moved before the pills are taken.

* *Sheetapitta* (urticaria) can be cured by applying Tulsi juice in which finely powdered saindhav rock salt has been dissolved.

* In cases of smallpox and of *romanti,* a disease akin to smallpox, once the fever has subsided and the eruptions have appeared, application of a paste formed by grinding *ajwan* seeds in Tulsi juice is beneficial.

* Dressing a wound with a warm paste of ground Tulsi seeds heals the wound, and the concomitant swelling with decolorization also subsides.

* Drinking the juice of the leaves of Ram Tulsi regularly proves beneficial in serious diseases like leprosy, if the treatment is continued for the period of about a year.

* The pain in the initial stages of measles, chickenpox and smallpox is alleviated by drinking the extract of Van Tulsi.

* If suffering from dracontiasis, apply the paste obtained by rubbing Tulsi roots on a flat stone on the spots on the skin that are itching. This will have the effect of causing the worm-like organism to come out to the extent of two to three inches. Wind this portion of the worm on a suitable piece of twig like a thread in the usual way, and apply the paste again the next day. Repetition of this treatment for two or three days will cause the whole organism to emerge. The resulting wound will heal completely if the same treatment is continued.

* If blisters caused by poisons are washed with a hot extract of Tulsi leaves, the poison will be extracted and washed away.

* Organisms infesting wounds are destroyed by sprinkling finely powdered dry Tulsi leaves on and around the wounds.

* The juice of fresh Tulsi leaves can also be used in place of powdered dry leaves in the above treatment.

* Dry some Tulsi roots, and grind them to powder. This powder taken with betel leaves is beneficial in leprosy.

* Itching and eczema can be cured by applying a paste obtained by grinding the leaves of a Tulsi plant in lemon juice.

* The discomfort caused by prickly heat can be relieved by eating Tulsi seeds with five grammes of *anvla* (Indian gooseberry) jam.

* If there is a swelling, apply crushed Tulsi leaves over the affected part.

* Swelling will also subside if a paste obtained by crushing Tulsi leaves and *makoy (kakamachi)* leaves is applied.

* A patient suffering from tetanus should be made to drink five grammes of mixture of the juices of garlic, ginger, onions and the leaves of Shyam Tulsi. The mixture of juices should also be applied all over his body. This treatment will cure tetanus.

14. DISEASES OF THE DIGESTIVE SYSTEM

* Drinking 10 to 20 grammes of Tulsi juice sweetened with a little crystal sugar and spiced with a pinch of powdered cardamom seeds and a pinch of powdered cloves is beneficial in cases of vomiting. Alternatively the juice can be taken with honey and lemon juice.

* A mixture of Tulsi and ginger juices with little honey will also be of benefit in such cases.

* Vomiting caused by excess of bile subsides in drinking a mixture of 10 grammes of Tulsi juice, 10 grammes of ginger juice and 20 grammes of lemon juice sweetened with powdered sugar.

DISEASES OF THE DIGESTIVE SYSTEM

* Taking two grammes of the powdered seeds of small cardamoms and 10 grammes of sugar mixed with 10 grammes of Tulsi juice will also cause vomiting to subside, including vomiting caused by the joint action of the two humours *vata* and *pitta*.

* Vomiting resulting from the concerted action of excessive *vata, pitta* and *kapha* can be cured by drinking Tulsi juice to which powdered cardamom seeds have been added.

* Drinking 5 grammes of Tulsi juice with 2 grammes of *gopi chandan* will cure vomiting. If one such dose does not have the desired effect, the dose should be repeated.

* Vomiting ceases on chewing Tulsi leaves with cardamom seeds.

* Vomiting and lack of appetite are cured by taking a mixture of powdered *peepar* (piper longum) and powdered Tulsi seeds with honey.

* Taking cinnamon powder in Tulsi leaf juice is beneficial in cases of vomiting.

* Vomiting of all types subsides on taking Tulsi juice with honey.

* Tulsi seeds taken with cow's milk will be of benefit in cases of vomiting.

* Take 5 grammes each of Tulsi leaves, sugar and the kernels of the stones of the fruits of *zizyphus jujuba,* i.e., jujubes or *ber* fruits. Add 2 grammes of black pepper seeds. Grind all these together, add little water and roll the resulting paste into pea-sized pills. Taking two of these pills in the mornings and two in the evenings will prove beneficial in cases of vomiting.

* Drinking a mixture of 10 grammes of Tulsi juice and 25 grammes of water sweetened with 10 grammes of sugar cures vomiting caused by fever.

* In case of poor digestion, drink 20 grammes of ginger juice with an equal amount of Tulsi juice, and take the same

mixture again after some time. A suspension of 2.5 grammes of powdered *peepari mool* (piper longum roots) in 20 grammes of Tulsi juice can be taken instead of the above mixture.

* Drinking 25 grammes of a mixture of the juices of Tulsi leaves and leaves of the drumstick tree with a little saindhav salt will stimulate digestion and will also induce a satisfactory bowel motion.

* If suffering from lack of appetite and poor digestion, mix one teaspoonful of Tulsi juice, one teaspoonful of ginger juice, half a teaspoonful of lemon juice and half a teaspoonful of honey, and lick this mixture (without additional water) some time prior to meals.

* The dried *panchang* (five parts) of the Tulsi plant, and black pepper seeds, powdered according to the prescribed procedure and taken with warm water will cure poor digestion and other disorders of the digestive system.

* Take 10 grammes of Tulsi juice, 10 grammes of powdered dry ginger, 20 grammes of aged jaggery. Grind them together and roll into pea-sized pills. Taking one of these pills with hot water every morning, noon and evening will cure dyspepsia, poor digestion and allied disorders.

* Take 10 grammes of each of the following ingredients : dried Tulsi leaves, seeds of large cardamoms, cumin seeds, dry ginger, cinnamon, *ajwan* seeds, black salt and roasted asafoetida. Pulverize these ingredients together and sieve the resulting powder. Taking this powder with water stimulates digestive powers.

* Digestion is stimulated by chewing five leaves of the Tulsi plant after the mid-day meal, or indeed at any other time.

* Drinking Tulsi decoction to which some saindhav salt and powdered dry ginger have been added, cures constipation.

* Drinking 10 grammes of Tulsi juice mixed with 5 grammes of honey and 5 grammes of powdered black pepper is a good remedy for poor digestion.

* Take 10 grammes of Tulsi juice, 10 grammes of dry ginger powder and 20 grammes of aged jaggery. Mix them well and roll into pea-sized pills. One of these pills taken three times a day will cure dyspepsia, poor digestion and allied disorders of the digestive system.

* Equal quantities of 'white' (Ram) Tulsi, *guruch* (serpent stone), *apamarg (latjeeta)* seeds, *indrajav,* the inner bark of the neem tree, and the fruit of the *karanj* creeper are boiled with water to prepare a decoction. Drinking this decoction in a quantity greater than that required to fill the stomach (literally, "till the liquid level rises to the level of the throat") will induce vomiting, thus relieving the discomfort caused by *vilambica* i.e., constipation.

* Drinking 10 grammes of Tulsi leaf juice and 2 grammes of black salt with hot water is an effective remedy for dyspepsia.

* Ingestion of equal quantities of Tulsi leaves and powdered black pepper not only cures dyspepsia, but also proves beneficial in cholera.

* Licking equal quantities of powdered Tulsi seeds and powdered *peepar* (piper longum) with honey will stimulate appetite.

* Take equal quantities of the roots of the Tulsi plant and the stones of the fruits of the neem tree. Grind these together and prepare pea-sized pills out of the resulting paste. Two of these pills taken with honey every morning and evening will cure piles. The pills can be taken with buttermilk instead of honey.

* Piles can also be cured by taking 10 grammes of powdered Tulsi leaves every morning and evening with water.

* The pain caused by piles can be alleviated by smearing them with the juice of Tulsi leaves.

* Drinking the juice of equal quantities of Tulsi leaves and the roots of *kakjangha (arun),* and application of the juice on the painful sores of piles, affords relief.

* Piles can be cured by regular ingestion of Tulsi in various forms, and application of its juice on the incipient outgrowths, or exerescences.

* If excess of bile causes a feeling of nausea, take 10 grammes of Tulsi seeds with *anvla* (Indian gooseberry) jam.

* If there is a burning sensation in the chest, the stomach or the calves, application of a paste of Tulsi leaves mixed with a paste obtained by rubbing a piece of *deodar* wood on a flat stone (like sandalwood) gives relief.

* If red sore patches are formed on the skin due to abnormal amount of bile in the body, the ingestion of 10 grammes of Tulsi seeds with *anvla* jam is beneficial.

* Take equal quantities of Tulsi inflorescences, bark of the neem tree, black pepper and *peepar* (piper longum) and pulverize them together. Five grammes of this powder taken with fresh water every morning will ameliorate the condition known as *amla-pitta,* i.e., hyperacidity caused by bile.

* Two grammes of each of the following ingredients are taken :

Tulsi inflorescences, *peepar* (piper longum), dry ginger, cloves, the stems of betel leaves, cinnamon, raisins and dates. Add one gramme of *lodh,* and prepare a decoction by boiling with water. Taking such a decoction regularly will cure not only acidity, but also excessive persistent thirst, burning sensation, depression and disorders caused by all the three humours *(vata, pitta* and *kapha)* jointly. The decoction should be taken four times daily.

* Burning sensation in the stomach due to excess of bile is relieved by drinking an extract of Tulsi leaves prepared by boiling 10 grammes of the leaves in 250 grammes of water till only half of the water remains, cooling the liquid, and sweetening it with sugar.

* Taking 10 grammes of Tulsi juice affords relief in *Rasajadaah,* i.e., burning sensation resulting from the ingestion of mercury or of formulations containing mercury.

* Drinking cardamom and mint powders with Tulsi juice cures diarrhoea.

* A decoction of the *panchang* (five parts) of the Tulsi plant regularizes bowel motions and augments digestive powers.

* Drinking the above decoction after adding 3 grammes of powdered nutmeg brings rapid relief even in difficult cases of irregularity in bowel motions.

* Take equal quantities of Tulsi leaves, *mandar* roots and black pepper. Grind these ingredients together and roll into pills. These pills constitute an effective remedy for cholera.

* Diarrhoea can be cured by regular daily ingestion of a mixture of 2 grammes of powdered dry Tulsi leaves and 5 grammes of *isabgul* (white cumin seeds).

* Taking 5 dried leaves of Tulsi and 2 grammes of black salt in 50 grammes of curds is highly beneficial in the treatment of dysentery or diarrhoea.

* Another effective treatment for dysentery is the administration of the powder of dried Tulsi leaves with equal quantities of cumin seeds and black salt in curds, or *mattha* (curds from which the whey has been drained).

* Take two grammes of each of the following ingredients :

Tulsi seeds, seeds of the larger variety of cardamoms, *bilva* (Bael) fruit and *saunf* (fenel seeds). Grind them together to a fine powder, divide into eight equal parts, and prepare eight packets from these portions. Take one such packet every morning and one every evening with buttermilk prepared from cow's milk, sweetened with jaggery.

* Take equal quantities of these ingredients : Tulsi leaves, black pepper, *ajwan* seeds, garlic, saindhav salt and pure camphor. Grind the ingredients together, and roll the resulting paste into pills of the size of Bengal grams. These pills are effective in the treatment of dysentery.

* Soak 10 grammes of Tulsi seeds in 50 grammes of water. Leave them to soak overnight. Grind the seeds in the same

water in the morning and strain the suspension. Drink the suspension with milk or water. This treatment cures 'raktatisar', diarrhoea in which blood is passed with the stools.

* Take 10 grammes of each of these ingredients : Tulsi leaves, jujube (ber) stone kernels, and pulp of the bilwa fruit. Add 5 grammes of black pepper, and a little water. Grind to a paste and roll into pea-sized pills. Two of these pills taken three times a day with mattha (drained curds) prepared from cow's milk will cure diarrhoea.

* Tulsi leaves and the bark of the indrajav plant powdered together, or an extract of the mixed powder will cure diarrhoea of the type described as 'pravahika', in which copious thin watery stools are passed.

* Diarrhoea due to inefficient digestion is cured by administering an extract of Tulsi leaves, to which the powder of saunf (fenel seeds) fried in ghee prepared from cow's milk, and sugar have been added.

* Administration of a spoonful of Tulsi juice mixed with a spoonful or turmeric juice three times a day is beneficial in any disorder of the digestive system.

* If suffering from recurring stomach ulcers or flatulence, prepare a decoction of Tulsi leaves and the leafy part of the sova (soya, dill) plant, add a little saindhav salt, and drink it up.

* Grind together equal quantities of Tulsi roots, salammoniac, borax (the dehydrated form), and javakhar (yavakshar). If suffering from progressive enlargement of the spleen, take five grammes of the above powder with fresh water every day.

* Ghee, Tulsi juice and black pepper are taken in equal quantities and ground together. Ten grammes of the resulting mixture taken every morning destroys all abnormalities of vata (vayu). The mixture can be taken with honey if so desired.

DISEASES OF THE DIGESTIVE SYSTEM

* If suffering from sharp pains in the flanks, chest or stomach, grind together 2 grammes of *ajwan* seeds, 2 grammes of the roots of *peepar* (piper longum), and 2 grammes of soda bicarb, and swallow the mixed powder with a little water. Take two teaspoonfuls of Tulsi leaf juice after that.

* Prolapse of the rectum caused by flatulence and constipation will be cured by an extract of Tulsi leaves. Taking essence of Tulsi regularly is also helpful.

* Ten grammes of Shyam Tulsi, 5 grammes of *nagod (nirgundi)*, 10 grammes of *bhringraj* and two grammes of *vayvarna* are powdered together. All disorders caused by abnormalities of *vata (vayu)* can be cured by taking 5 grammes of this powder daily with honey.

* Ingestion of 10 grammes of the juice of fresh Tulsi leaves every morning is beneficial in cases of dyspepsia and constipation.

* Drinking a warmed mixture of equal quantities of the juices of Tulsi and ginger cures stomachache.

* Chewing Tulsi leaves with a little sugar is a good remedy for colic.

* If suffering from stomachache, drink 10 grammes of the juice of fresh Tulsi leaves.

* Five grammes of powdered Tulsi leaves, five grammes of roasted cumin seeds, five grammes of *bili (bilwa)* powder and two grammes of black salt are added to 50 grammes of curds, and mixed well. This mixture is beneficial in dysentery, colic, grips and inefficient digestion.

* Swallowing eleven leaves of Tulsi ground with two grammes of *vavding (vay-vidang)* in water every morning and evening will kill worms infesting the stomach.

* Worms in the stomach are also killed by the ingestion of fresh Tulsi leaf juice.

* If troubled by worms in the digestive tract, take a warmed mixture of 10 grammes of Tulsi leaf juice and 10 grammes of ginger juice three times a day.

* Worms in the stomach are killed by the ingestion of 10 grammes of warmed Tulsi juice with two grammes of powdered black pepper and 10 grammes of powdered *vavding (vay-vidang)*.

* Inflammation will subside if a paste obtained by grinding together 10 grammes each of the leaves of the Tulsi plant and the leaves of *makoy (kakamachi)* is applied over the affected area.

* Persistent thirst is relieved by drinking Tulsi juice and lemon juice mixed with water sweetened with sugar.

* Diarrhoea is cured by swallowing 25 grammes of powdered Tulsi seeds with 25 grammes of sugar. Treatment with a mixture of the juice of Tulsi leaves, the juice of the leaves of the *bili (bilwa)* tree, and the juice of pepper of a few days will also cure diarrhoea.

* Boil 10 grammes of Tulsi leaves in 100 grammes of water, till only half the water is left, and strain the extract. Drinking this extract will arrest the enlargement of the liver, and cure allied disorders.

* Soak 10 grammes of Tulsi seeds in 100 grammes of water overnight. Crush the seeds well in the same water in the morning. Add sugar. Drinking the suspension is beneficial in dysuria.

* Prepare a decoction of Tulsi inflorescences. Seat a patient suffering from bladder stones on a chair. Place an *angeethi* (a coal stove) under the chair, and put the vessel containing the decoction on the stove. Expose the urinary organ of the patient to the steam rising from the decoction for some time. Frequent steaming in this manner will have the effect of breaking the stones and dissolving them, resulting in removal of the stones without surgery.

* Daily ingestion of five grammes of Tulsi powder with five grammes of sugar cures diarrhoea.

* Drinking Tulsi leaf juice and applying it externally every day will cure all disorders of the liver and the spleen.

* Applying a paste of ground Tulsi leaves will cure inflammations.

* Drinking an extract of Tulsi seeds and *sona mukhi* leaves is a cure for *aanaah*, i.e., obstruction in the urinary tract and the rectum.

* Application of a paste prepared by grinding together Tulsi seeds, white *sarasao (sarason)*, radish seeds, drumstick seeds, barley and the roots of *kaner* cures tumours.

* Hiccups can be cured by taking a teaspoonful of Tulsi juice and half a spoonful of honey in the morning and evening.

* Take equal quantities of Tulsi, dry ginger, *mulethi (yashti madhu), guruch* (serpent stone) and *chitraphala*. Prepare an extract of these ingredients. This extract is an effective cure for hiccups.

* Prepare an extract of equal quantities of Tulsi leaves and Tulsi inflorescences. Mix aged jaggery well with the extract. Taking the mixture regularly will cure hiccups.

15. DISEASES OF THE MOUTH, TEETH, EYES, EARS, NOSE AND THROAT

* If there are ulcers in the mouth, chewing Tulsi and chameli leaves is beneficial.

* Chewing four or five leaves of Tulsi two to four times a day, especially after meals, will clean the mouth, remove bad odours emanating from the mouth and get rid of a bad taste in the mouth. A regular use of Tulsi will in fact cure all disorders of the mouth.

* Gargling with a decoction of the *panchang* (five parts) of the Tulsi plant affords protection from disorders of the teeth such as decay, cures any disorder of the teeth that has been contracted previously, and kills the micro-organisms infesting the teeth.

* Toothache is alleviated by rubbing the teeth with the juice of Tulsi leaves mixed with black pepper powder and salt.

* Placing a pill made from the paste of Tulsi leaves under an aching tooth will also alleviate the pain. Pills rolled from a paste prepared by grinding black pepper with the juice of Tulsi leaves are also effective. Pressing a paste of Tulsi leaves and black pepper on an aching tooth will also relieve toothache.

* The *panchang* of the Tulsi plant, betel nuts and almond shells are first roasted in a pan till they are charred, and then powdered. Fifty grammes of this powder is mixed with a finely powdered mixture of 10 grammes of black pepper, 10 grammes of camphor, 10 grammes of cloves, 10 grammes of alum, 10 grammes of *mulethi (yashti madhu),* and 10 grammes of *peepal* catechu. Brushing the teeth with this tooth powder every morning will reset loose teeth firmly in the gums. The powder is beneficial in pyorrhoea and in fact any disorder of the teeth.

* Grind Tulsi leaves, camphor and cloves together to a paste and roll into pills. Keeping these pressed under the teeth affords relief in pyorrhoea and other disorders of the teeth.

* Brushing the teeth with the powder of dried Tulsi leaves is beneficial.

* Take 10 grammes of each of the following ingredients :

Dry Tulsi leaves, *akkalgaro* (palatory root), *jatamansi* (spikenard), *saindhav* salt, ashes *(bhasma)* of almond shells, roasted betel nut, and *Roomi* (Roman) gum. Add 5 grammes of cardamom seeds. Grind to powder. Use this powder to brush the teeth every morning and evening, and also after meals if desired. This is another tooth powder that is beneficial in all disorders of the teeth, including pyorrhoea.

* Prepare a decoction of the leaves of Shyam Tulsi, dissolve some alum in it, and strain it. If wads of cotton are wetted with this decoction and placed on the eyelids, eye strain is relieved, swelling of the eyelids subsides and vision is improved.

* Night blindness can be cured by instilling two drops of the juice of Shyam Tulsi leaves into the eyes every day for fourteen days.

* Grind 5 grammes of Tulsi seeds, 5 grammes of *raswanti*, 5 grammes of mango ginger and 2 grammes of opium with the pulp of *kunvarpatha*. Applying this paste around the eyes alleviates pain.

* Dropping Tulsi juice into the eyes relieves soreness of the eyes and is also beneficial in other eye disorders. Tulsi juice mixed with honey, strained and stored in a glass bottle, constitutes excellent medicinal eye-drops.

* Prepare a decoction of Tulsi leaves and dissolve some powdered alum in the decoction. If there is inflammation or itching of the eyelids, warm this decoction and use cotton dipped into it to foment the eyelids. During the fomentation, change the cotton wads twice in every five minutes. The swelling will subside, and it will become possible to open the eyes without discomfort.

* Take equal quantities of Tulsi, turmeric, white *sarasao (sarason), bhangaro (bhringraj)* and indigo. Grind to a paste. Application of this paste benefits the eyes.

* Take plenty of Tulsi leaves and cook them in *sarason* oil. When the leaves have blackened due to charring, take the oil off the fire and strain it. Instillation of two drops of this oil into the ears is beneficial in disorders of the ears.

* Boil Tulsi leaves and whole (unbroken) seeds of black pepper in *til* (seasame) oil, and strain the oil. Instilling this oil into the ears cures deafness, and suppuration of the ears.

* Mix Tulsi juice with seasame oil and boil the mixture. A few drops of this oil instilled into the ears while still bearably hot will cure all disorders of the ears.

* Pain in the external ear is alleviated to a considerable extent by massaging with Tulsi leaf juice.

* Instillation of a mixture of equal amounts of the juices of Shyam Tulsi leaves and *Bhringraj* is an effective treatment for infection of the internal ear and consequent suppuration.

* Earache, inflammation of the inner ear and deafness are cured by regularly instilling drops of the mixed juice of green Tulsi inflorescences and Tulsi leaves.

* Deafness can also be cured by instilling into the ears the juice of Van Tulsi leaves strained through cloth.

* Instilling Tulsi leaf juice into the ears will cure earache, including sharp, shooting pains in the ears. If there is pus formation, the ears should first be cleaned and two drops of Tulsi juice should be instilled into each ear. This should be repeated every morning and evening. Warming the juice a little before using it is permissible.

* Earache is alleviated by instilling a mixture of the juices of Tulsi leaves and maize leaves.

* If a furuncle has formed in the nose, inhalation of a pinch of dry powdered Tulsi leaves like snuff will prove beneficial.

* If the nasal passages are infected with micro-organisms due to dacryocystitis, with consequent emanation of bad odour, the vapours from a mixture of Tulsi leaf juice and camphor should be inhaled.

* Another effective treatment for bad odour originating in the nasal passages is the inhalation of the vapours emanating

from seasame oil in which Tulsi, dry ginger, pepper, *peepar (piper longum), vachh,* drumstick, the smaller variety of *danti, chitraphala* and *saindhav* salt have been cooked. Drops of such oil instilled into the nostrils are also effective.

* If there is pain in the nasal passages or a furuncle has developed in the passages, a mixture of powdered Tulsi leaves and powdered kernels of the stones of the jujube *(ber)* fruit should be inhaled, and the mixed powder should also be applied on the affected area.

* In case of organisms infesting the nostrils, the juice of fresh Tulsi leaves instilled into the nostrils will destroy them.

* A nosebleed can be stanched by repeatedly inhaling the medicinal vapours given off by Tulsi inflorescences.

* The juice of Tulsi leaves mixed with honey and licked without additional water is beneficial in case of sore throat.

16. DISEASES OF THE HEART, FLANKS, HEAD AND OTHER MISCELLANEOUS DISEASES

* Take 5 grammes of Tulsi leaves and 5 grammes of the roots of the *brahmi* plant. Grind them to powder. Stir the powder into a glassful of water, strain the suspension, and add sugar. This drink strengthens memory. It is also beneficial in cases of mental disorders like hysteria, mania, etc. If taken every day, the drink confers great benefits.

* Rub Tulsi roots on a flat stone like sandalwood, and apply the resulting paste over the forehead. This will alleviate headache, and relieve mental tension.

* If pains develop in the heart, chewing eight or ten leaves of Tulsi with two or three black pepper seeds will produce a magical effect.

* If there is pain in the flanks, chest or heart, drink 10 to 20 grammes of Tulsi juice, and massage the affected part with the juice. Grind Tulsi leaves to a paste and apply the paste too over the painful areas. The pain will subside. (Tulsi has been given the very appropriate appellation of 'shoolaghni', the destroyer of pain, in Ayurveda, because of its ability to remove pain.)

* Regular daily ingestion of finely powdered dried Tulsi roots will cure disorders of the brain and the nerves.

* Inhaling the smoke formed when the inflorescences of Van Tulsi and black pepper are sprinkled on glowing coals will cure a headache.

* If someone loses consciousness, a few drops of Tulsi juice instilled into his nostrils will restore consciousness.

* Headache can be cured by drinking half a spoonful of Tulsi juice mixed with half a spoonful of lemon juice.

* Even when one is in a healthy condition, taking 8–10 Tulsi leaves with four or five black pepper seeds ground to a fine powder every day in the morning proves beneficial. The brain is rendered more efficient. Two to four almonds and a little honey can be taken with the powder.

* If one takes five leaves of Tulsi with water after the morning bath, any weakness of the brain is removed, and both memory and intellectual capacity are increased.

* Pain in the flanks is cured by applying a thick layer of the warmed and thickened paste formed by grinding the roots of the *pushkar* plant with the juices of Tulsi and ginger.

* Heart disease can be cured by taking 2 grammes of powdered Tulsi leaves with 4 grammes of the powdered bark of the *Arjun* tree.

* The deposition of fats can be arrested by taking Tulsi juice mixed with honey regularly every day for some time.

* Massage with a thin paste of ground fresh Tulsi leaves is of great benefit in cases of epilepsy. This treatment should be given regularly over a period of many days at a stretch.

* If 5-6 leaves of Tulsi crushed with 3-4 black pepper seeds are taken in an empty stomach regularly for 21 days, the brain is strengthened and soothed, the 'heat' contained in it being removed by the treatment.

* A paste formed by rubbing a little camphor on a flat stone with Tulsi juice and applied on the forehead, like sandalwood paste, relieves headache immediately. Pain in the external ear or in the region behind the ear is also alleviated by the application of a warmed paste of equal parts of Tulsi and tender shoots of the castor oil plant crushed together, with some saindhav salt.

* **For improving memory :** (1) Swallow five leaves of the Tulsi plant with water every morning. (2) Crush together 8 to 10 Tulsi leaves, 4-5 black pepper seeds, 2-4 almonds and a little honey. Regular ingestion of this preparation greatly improves the powers of the brain.

* **Purification of polluted water :** Polluted water is purified and sanctified by dropping a few fresh green Tulsi leaves in it.

* **Treatment for electric shock :** If a person has received an electric shock either by touching a wire carrying an electric current, or by lightning, massage the face and the head of the victim with Tulsi juice. This will restore him to consciousness.

* **Treatment of burns :** Smear the affected part with coconut oil that has previously been boiled with Tulsi juice. This will reduce the pain and will hasten the subsidence of the blisters and the healing of the wounds.

* **Freeing oneself from addiction to betel leaves :** The habit of chewing betel leaves results in weakening of the gums and deterioration of the teeth. Tulsi leaves can be used to free oneself from the habit. If you are addicted to the habit of taking betel leaves after meals, you may take the betel leaf after a meal, but follow it up by chewing a few Tulsi leaves. This will clean and freshen the mouth, and remove any bad

odours originating in the mouth. The digestion is improved. In Shri Lanka there is a tradition of using Tulsi leaves as we use betel leaves : applying lime and catechu, enfolding coarse betel nut powder in them, and chewing them as we chew betel leaves. Adoption of this method of cleaning the mouth would free one from addiction to betel leaves.

* **Curing hereditary diseases :** It is considered almost impossible to cure or prevent hereditary diseases. In this matter allopathic treatment is avowedly ineffective. Other systems of medicine have also failed. But Tulsi possesses a special capacity to free the body from all abnormalities. There is no difficulty in curing even hereditary diseases. It is clearly stated in 'Padmapurana' that if the woody trunk of Tulsi, or clay in which a Tulsi plant is growing, is rubbed like sandalwood on a flat stone, and the resulting paste smeared regularly on the forehead, the process of curing hereditary diseases is assisted to a very great extent.

* **Persistent thirst :** Persistent, excessive thirst will be quenched satisfactorily by drinking the *sherbet* (sweet soft drink) prepared by adding sugar and lemon juice to the juice of Tulsi leaves.

* **For strengthening the heart :** The heart can be strengthened by regular daily ingestion of 5-7 leaves of Tulsi, 3-4 black pepper seeds and 3-4 almonds. This treatment should be taken throughout the winter season every year.

* **Fainting :** Add some *saindhav* salt to Tulsi juice and boil it well. Instilling 2-4 drops of this juice into the nostrils will restore a person who has fainted to consciousness.

* **Tuberculosis :** Careful and conscientious treatment with Tulsi can ensure recovery from Tuberculosis from the very first stage. There was in ancient time a tradition of establishing vast Tulsi sanatoria. These sanatoria had Tulsi Vans, miniature forests of Tulsi plants, in their grounds. There were sanitary huts, the walls and floors of which were plastered with clay in which Tulsi plants had been growing. The sole aim of this

plaster was to ensure that the TB germs should not be able to get a foothold in the walls or the floor. The volatile oil present in Tulsi leaves destroys these germs. Thus it can be ensured that effective assistance is given by various methods of using Tulsi in curing Tuberculosis.

* Tulsi is a highly efficacious remedy for anaemia. Regular use of Tulsi effects a very rapid increase in the number of the red blood corpuscles.

* All kinds of wounds heal quickly and even broken bones join very rapidly when treated suitably with Tulsi.

* Allopathic doctors have no cure for chronic migraine. But regular treatment with Tulsi will cure it.

* Regular use of Tulsi maintains our health and protects us from a large number of infectious diseases.

* Cut dried twigs or stems of Tulsi plants with scissors into beads of the size of large pearls. Sort the pieces according to different sizes. String together beads of a uniform size with the help of a needle, or get them set in a gold or a silver chain. Wearing such a necklace of Tulsi beads protects one from infectious diseases, as the germs of the diseases cannot come near the wearer.

* Swallowing five leaves of Tulsi every morning also protects one from infectious diseases. (But care should be taken to ensure that they do not come in contact with the teeth, as such contact will harm the enamel of the teeth.)

* During an epidemic, arrange to administer one spoonful of a mixture of the juices of Tulsi leaves and neem leaves to every member of your family twice every day, once in the morning and once in the evening. This will ensure the safety of your family.

* The leaves of Van Tulsi exhibit wonderful efficacy in the treatment of cholera. Take 20-30 grammes of each of the following ingredients :

Tulsi leaves, kernels of the seeds of *kanaji,* the bark of the neem tree, *adhedi (latjeera)* seeds, *guruchi (amrita)* from the neem tree, and *indrajav.* Boil them in half a litre of water till half the water has been boiled away. Give the cholera patient 20-30 grammes of this extract at short intervals. This treatment ensures the survival of cholera patients in almost all cases.

* Tulsi leaf juice sweetened with sugar is a good preventive for sunstroke, and if one already has got sunstroke, the drink will assist recovery.

* Breathing in the vicinity of a Tulsi plant cures diseases of the lungs and energises (strengthens) the lungs.

* Drinking an extract of Ram Tulsi leaves with cow's milk and sugar removes fatigue instantly, and imparts a feeling of freshness and cheer.

* Things exposed to the aroma of Tulsi or placed near a Tulsi plant will not deteriorate or get spoiled quickly. A dead body, too, does not decay rapidly if placed among Tulsi plants. Perhaps the religious ritual of putting Tulsi leaves in the mouth of a dead person or keeping a Tulsi plant near a dead body originated on the basis of this fact.

17. TULSI : PREPARATION OF MEDICINAL FORMULATIONS

Tulsi Tea : Wash 10 to 20 fresh leaves of Tulsi, and pound them to a pulp. Mix this pulp with a cupful of water. Spice the mixture with proper amounts of powdered dry ginger, cardamom seeds and roots of *peepar (piper longum).* Add a spoonful of sugar, and boil. Drink this decoction while still hot. Do not strain the decoction. Chew and swallow the cooked pulp of Tulsi leaves after drinking the decoction. Take this decoction every morning. This decoction, which can be described as Tulsi tea, is believed to be capable of curing various diseases, stimulating appetite, and imparting a feeling of freshness and vigour. In order to take advantage of the beneficial qualities of Tulsi, make it a rule to take the decoction every morning. Substitution of this Tulsi tea for the usual morning tea is especially beneficial during the winter.

Alternatively, 10 grammes of Tulsi leaves are boiled in 250 grammes of water till only half or one-fourth of the water remains. An equal amount of milk is added, and 20 to 25 grammes of crystal sugar dissolved in it, the amount being adjusted as needed. Tulsi tea prepared thus is not only a palatable drink, but also an effective cure for a number of disorders such as colds, fevers, lack of appetite, lassitude, burning sensation in the stomach, excess of *vata* and *pitta*, etc.

Boiling 10 grammes or more of Tulsi leaves in 250 grammes of water till one-half or one-quarter of the water has been boiled away yields another kind of Tulsi tea which is very effective in the treatment of disorders like fevers, a disinclination for exertion, lassitude, lack of appetite, burning sensation in the stomach and disorders caused by excess of *vata (vayu)* and *pitta*.

If an extract of Tulsi leaves is prepared as described above, an equal amount of milk is mixed with it, and 10 to 20 grammes of powdered *sudhamooli* and the powdered seeds of one or two cardamoms are added to it, a highly nutritious drink is obtained. The drink freshens the mouth, and cures a number of disorders.

Tea prepared from Tulsi leaves as indicated here is a thousand times better than tea prepared in the conventional foreign way, which lacks nutritional value and affects blood adversely.

Take 1500 grammes of Tulsi leaves dried in the shade. Add 500 grammes of *brahmi* roots, 1 kilogramme of *tamalpatra,* 1 kilogramme of powdered sandalwood, 1500 grammes of *aagia* grass, 250 grammes of cinnamon, 1 kilogramme of *saunf* (fenel seeds), 125 grammes of *banafashah,* and 500 grammes of cardamom seeds. Pulverize all these to a fine powder, and store in a glass jar.

When a hot tea-like drink is desired, boil 500 grammes of water, add 10 to 15 grammes of the above powder, and continue to boil till a homogeneous liquid is obtained. Strain the liquid and add sugar and milk according to your taste. This tea will be found highly beneficial in fevers, coughs, colds, excessive secretion of phlegm and disorders of the throat.

Cold extract of Tulsi : Grind five to seven leaves of Tulsi with three or four black pepper seeds in mortar with a little water till a homogeneous thick liquid is obtained. Drinking a glass of such a cold extract of Tulsi every morning in an empty stomach soothes the brain by removing 'heat', and strengthens it. This drink stimulates and strenghtens the heart also. The drink is more desirable in the cold season. Almonds added to the drink improve its quality and render it more salubrious.

Vegetable soup : Clean and cut four bundles of onion saplings, including the leaves, into small pieces. Keep these other ingredients ready : Water, 3 cups; Celery leaves cut into small pieces, 1 cup; diced carrots, 1 cup; skinned and diced tomatoes (of the larger variety); 3 nos.; 1 capsicum cut into small pieces, salt and pepper according to taste, some neem leaves, one spoonful of *ajwan* seeds, one spoonful of Tulsi, one spoonful of oregano.

Method of preparation : Fry the pieces of onion and capsicum in a little oil. Then add the rest of the ingredients and cook till they are done.

If it is desired to thicken the soup, cook a cupful of *phanasi* or other beans, mash them and add the paste to the soup. Add one-fourth of a cup of rice to the soup and boil till the rice is cooked.

Mixed pulse soup :

Ingredients : 250 grammes of dry pulse seeds (such as French beans, Bengal grams, string beans, lentils, etc.); 3 carrots of ordinary size, diced; one potato of average size, diced; one pumpkin, peeled and diced; 2 medium-sized tomatoes cut into slices or pieces; broken noodles; onions, garlic, and green pepper cut into pieces and fried, according to taste; and salt and pepper according to taste.

Two spoonfuls of celery leaves; one spoonful of oregano; half a spoonful of *ajwan* seeds; half a spoonful of Tulsi leaves or *tamalpatra;* one spoonful of jaggery; one spoonful of *ajwan* leaves; some neem leaves.

Method of preparation : Soak the pulses overnight, and cook in a pressure cooker till they become soft. Mash them in the water used for cooking them. Now add the rest of the vegetables and heat till they are cooked well. Decorate with celery leaves, *ajwan* leaves or Tulsi leaves when the soup is served.

Potato soup : White cream sauce (prepared by mixing 1 spoonful of butter, two spoonfuls of flour, 1 cup of milk, 1 cup cooked vegetables, salt and pepper according to taste) : 1 cup boiled, peeled and diced potatoes; 1 spoonful of *ajwan* seeds or oregano; 1 spoonful of Tulsi, 1 cup of parsley leaves or the leaves of onion saplings cut suitably (for decoration).

Mix some flour with the cooked vegetables to form a paste. Heat on a low flame and add the remaining vegetables and milk in small portions. Now add butter and boil till the soup thickens suitably.

Now apply cream to the boiled potatoes and the green leaves, add these to the soup and let it simmer. Decorate with parsley or onion leaves when you serve the soup.

A nutritious sweet (pak) prepared from Tulsi seeds : Tulsi seeds are used extensively in the preparation of medicines, eatables, essences, perfumes, antiseptics, etc. The seeds of the Shyam Tulsi are considered to be of greater medicinal value than those of Ram Tulsi. The clusters of flowers, or inflorescences, of the Tulsi plants are known as 'maanjars' (from 'manjari', inflorescence). The seeds are formed in these flowers, and are released from the dry maanjars on shaking. More seeds are produced by Ram Tulsi. The seeds are of the size of poppy seeds, and resemble mustard seeds in colour. The seeds are formed in abundance in the month of Ashvin, i.e., around October. A medicinal sweet which is nutritious and imparts strength to the body (i.e., a 'pak') can be prepared from these seeds.

Preparation : Pound or grind Tulsi seeds to a fine powder like flour. Before beginning the preparation, keep the following ingredients ready :

Tulsi seed flour, 125 grammes; black pepper seeds, 10 grammes; *bhang* (cannabis), 5 grammes; saffron, 2 grammes; almond seeds, 125 grammes; *khova (khoya)*, 125 grammes; Bengal gram flour, 125 grammes; crystal sugar, 250 grammes; ghee (clarified butter), 250 grammes.

Mix a major part of ghee with the gram flour. Sprinkle a little milk over the flour. Take the remaining portion of ghee in an iron or brass pan and put it on the stove. When ghee is fairly hot, add the gram flour and let it cook in ghee over a low flame. When the flour is nearly half-cooked, break up the khova into small lumps, mix it with the gram flour, and continue heating till both the khova and the flour have been cooked completely, and have begun to turn brown. Now add the almond seeds, cut into small pieces, and let them cook for some time. Now add the Tulsi seed flour. Immediately after that add the *cannabis* powder, cardamom and pepper powder according to your taste, mix well, and take the pan off the fire.

Meanwhile, prepare a thick syrup from the sugar, and add the saffron to it. The thickness of the syrup should be adjusted to suit the weather conditions. The thickness (or consistency) of the syrup should preferably be a little greater in monsoon, otherwise the sweet is liable to spoil easily, and become soft due to moisture in the air; a thicker syrup gives better result. In the winter, on the contrary, the syrup should not be made so thick and viscous; thicker syrup results in greater hardness of the sweet. If it is desired to increase the proportion of ghee in the sweet so as to increase its nutritive value, somewhat thinner syrup will be needed. Once the syrup of the proper consistency has been prepared, and the saffron added, mix the roasted flours into the syrup with constant stirring. Now the sweet is ready. Spread it in *a thali* or flat plate while it is still hot, and allow it to set. When it has set, cut it up into pieces of desired shape and size.

This *pak* should be taken every day in the morning. Depending on your constitution, 20 to 100 grammes of the sweet can be taken daily. The sweet should be followed up with 200 to 250 grammes of milk. It would be better not to take any oil, chillies, tamarind, hot spices and such other additives to one's food during the period of regular consumption of this *pak*, or at least reduce the proportion of these materials in the daily food. This will permit the *pak* to have its full effect on the body.

Benefits : It is stated in Ayurveda that Tulsi seeds are highly nutritious and greatly strengthen the body. The component of the body responsible for the strength and virility of the body is built up and the secretion of semen increases. Many diseases caused by *vata (vayu)* and *kapha* are cured. Digestion becomes more efficient. Numerous disorders including diseases of the digestive system, disorders caused by abnormal amounts of vata, wounds, weakening of the brain, chronic cold, cough, debility and dyspepsia are cured by taking this sweet regularly. Excessive diarrhoea is curbed. Those who suffer from chronic constipation derive considerable benefit if given this sweet mixed with powdered *nasotar* or powdered roots of *satodi (punarnava)*.

A refreshing drink : Pour one cup of boiling water into a teapot. Add 12 to 15 Tulsi leaves, two pieces of lemon grass (green tea), and 12 to 15 mint leaves. Allow to brew for 15 minutes, and strain. Add lemon juice and honey to improve the taste. Drink this decoction every morning on an empty stomach. It stimulates digestion, purifies the blood, and imparts a feeling of freshness. Honey is used for slimming and lemon juice for reducing the harm caused by the excess of bile. A piece of ginger can be added to the brew with advantage.

A digestive drink : Boil a cupful of water. Add two betel leaves cut into very thin short strips. Add a few Tulsi leaves and a teaspoonful of *ajwan* seeds. Let the water boil for some more time. When the liquid begins to thicken, take it off the fire. Grind the leaves in mortar with some of the liquid, and mix with the extract. Strain, and add a little honey. Add a little water to reduce the pungency and make the drink milder. Five to ten grammes of this drink taken every day for two or three days will stimulate the digestive powers and impart energy and vigour. Two spoonfuls of this liquid will suffice for children.

A health-giving sauce (chutney) :

Germinated green grams	20 grammes
Germinated Bengal grams	10 grammes
Germinated fenugreek seeds *(methi)*	5 grammes
Seasame seeds	5 grammes
Peanuts	5 grammes
Coriander leaves	10 grammes
Mint leaves	10 grammes
Tulsi leaves	5 grammes
Ginger	5 grammes
Garlic	5 grammes
Saindhav salt	5 grammes
Dates or jaggery	5 grammes

Grind all the above ingredients in a mortar to a fine paste. Add 15 grammes of shredded coconut and a teaspoonful of lemon juice. This chutney can be taken with chapaties, or it can even be mixed with vegetables. This chutney must be eaten within two hours after preparation. It begins to spoil after that time. Do not put it in the refrigerator. The chutney is a good source of calcium, potassium, sulphur, iron, proteins and enzymes.

This chutney is an effective remedy for constipation, acidity, gas, rheumatoid arthritis, obesity, diabetes, itching, burning sensation and many other disorders.

Arishta aasav : Pulverise 700 grammes of the bark of the *babool* tree. Boil it in 1500 grammes of water, till only one-fourth of the water is left. Strain the extract. Add 80 grammes of the *panchang* (five parts of the plant) of Tulsi, 500 grammes of jaggery, 10 grammes of *peepar (piper longum)*, and 80 grammes of flowers of the *anvla* (Indian gooseberry) plant. Take 10 grammes each of black pepper, small cardamoms, nutmeg, cinnamon, *sheetalchini* (cubebs), *tamalpatra* and *naag kesar* (iron wood). Pulverise them and mix with the above extract. Put this mixture in a vessel, and seal its mouth. Keep aside for one month, then open the vessel and strain the contents.

This *aasav* removes deficiencies of the semen such as a low sperm count and thinness. It also cures coughs, debility and poor digestion, and imparts strength and vigour.

Ghrit (medicated ghee) : Grind 125 grammes of Tulsi leaves and 125 grammes of *guruch* (serpent stone) in the presence of 750 grammes of water. Add 500 grammes of cow's *ghee* and boil till a homogeneous liquid is obtained. Strain and store the liquid.

This *ghrit* is used to treat abnormalities of the blood and skin diseases like leucoderma and leprosy.

Medicated oil : Grind 125 grammes of Tulsi leaves in mortar to a paste. Cook this paste in two kilogrammes of Tulsi juice to which one kilogramme of seasame oil has been added. Continue boiling till all the water is boiled away. Then cool the oil, strain it and store in a glass bottle. This oil is very useful in the treatment of skin diseases.

Choorna (medicinal powder) : Take equal quantities of the leaves, inflorescences, seeds, roots and stem of the Tulsi plant. Dry them in the shade. Then pulverize this *panchang*. Swallow 5 grammes of this *choorna* with cold water every morning. This *choorna* is useful in the treatment of abnormalities of the blood, disorders caused by *pitta,* insomnia and gonorrhoea.

Vayunashak choorna (powder for neutralizing excess of vata) : 25 grammes of Shyam Tulsi, 15 grammes of *nirgundi* roots, 25 grammes of *bhringraj,* 10 grammes of *malkangani* roots, 5 grammes of dry ginger, 5 grammes of black pepper, 5 grammes of the bark of the drumstick tree and 5 grammes of *peepar (piper longum)* : all these ingredients are ground together. The resulting powder is *vayunashak choorna.* Licking 5 grammes of this powder mixed with honey every morning and evening cures many disorders caused by excess of *vayu (vata).*

Sudarshanvati : Take 20 grammes of each of the following ingredients : Tulsi leaves, neem leaves, *guruch* (serpent stone), *vavding (vayvidang), bili (bilwa)* leaves, and *karanj* leaves. Add 10 grammes of sulphur and 10 grammes of camphor. Grind all these together, after adding *brahmi* juice, and roll the resulting paste into pea-sized pills. The proper doze of these pills is 2 pills for adults, and $\frac{1}{2}$ to 1 pill for children according to their ages. The use of these pills is very effective in the treatment of malaria, plague, itching due to abnormalities of the blood, marasmus, cholera, worms, etc.

Swadishta (pleasant-tasting) pills : Take 10 grammes of Tulsi leaves, 15 grammes of *javkhar (yav kshara),* 10 grammes of *peepar (piper longum),* 20 grammes of pomegranate seeds, 10 grammes of catechu and 10 grammes of *black pepper*. Pulverise all these, add 80 grammes of jaggery and prepare pea-sized pills out of the resulting paste. Put one of these pills in the mouth, and suck it like a linguet. This is beneficial in cases of cough and disorders of the throat.

Sheetajwarantakvati (pills that end malaria) : Pulverize 10 grammes of Tulsi leaves, 40 grammes of Bengal gram powder, 10 grammes of black pepper and 10 grammes of the leaves of the bitter gourd creeper. Add some water, mix and roll into pea-sized pills. Regular use of these pills in seasons favouring malaria will prevent an attack of the disease. Taking one of these pills three times a day, or two of them every morning and every evening, is beneficial in fevers preceded by cold rigours and fevers prevalent in winter. These pills should not be taken for periods longer than two months.

Choorna (powder) for colds : Pulverize *black pepper* to a fine powder which can pass through cloth. Subject the powder to the process described as *bhavna* with the help of Tulsi. Dry the powder in the shade. Five grammes of this powder should be taken with tea or hot water for treating colds.

18. TULSI : READYMADE FORMULATIONS

A large number of medicinal formulations incorporating Tulsi have been described in Ayurveda. Some of these formulations are being described here in order that the readers should come to know about formulations with the help of which they can enjoy long and healthy lives. All the preparations described here are available in ready-to-use forms at reasonable prices in all medical stores authorised to dispense Ayurvedic medicines.

A remedy for all disorders caused by vata (vayu) : 'Laghu Raajmrigank' is a formulation containing equal quantities of Tulsi juice, *ghee* prepared from cow's milk, and powdered *black pepper*. Regular use of this medicine cures nearly all acute diseases! Out of nearly eighty disorders resulting from abnormal formation of *vayu*, including paralysis, sciatica, poliomyelitis, arthritis, rheumatism, convulsions, tetanus, parkinsonism, fainting, epilepsy, total paralysis (paraplegia), hemiplegia, facial paralysis, enlargement of the prostate, flatulence, excessive formation of gas, colitis, headache, pain in the lower part of the spine, angina pectoris, pain in the flanks, pain in the nape, sharp shooting pains in the ears, spondylitis, stiffness of the arms, pain in any part of the body, or numbness of any of the limbs, stammering, degeneration of the body or of a limb, insomnia, oligosomnia, infertility due to abnormalities of the semen or of the menstrual cycle as a result of excess of *vayu*, fatigue, excessive proneness to yawning, and such other disorders can be cured by treatment with 'Laghu Raajmrigank'. The medicine is so harmless that there is absolutely no possibility of any adverse effect, since all the three ingredients of the formulation are ordinary harmless substances, and are in fact foods rather than medicines. (These medicine is not available in the market. It is therefore advisable to compound all the three elements to prepare it at home.)

Jwarasamharak (destroyer of fever) *rasa* : Dosage : Take two grammes of the *rasa* mixed with *godanti bhasma*, with either plain water or *jwaraghna* (fever-destroying) *kwath* (extract).

Benefits : The medicine is beneficial in case of any fever, especially influenza (flu) and malaria. The phlegm matures and gets expectorated when influenza is treated with this *rasa* mixed with *gojihwadi kwath*. Colds, orthopnea and coughs are also cured promptly. If there is pain in the flanks along with influenza, *jwarasamharak rasa* should be administered with the *bhasma* (ashes) of antelope horns. If the fever is due to pneumonia, the *rasa* should be given with five grammes of *shringa bhasma* and one gramme of *abhrak bhasma*. Follow that up with five grammes of *gojihvadi kashay* or *bhargyadi kashay,* and five grammes of *yavakshar. Jwarasamharak rasa* can be used to treat acute fevers as well as chronic fevers.

Tribhuvan keerti rasa : Dosage : One pill of the *rasa* three or four times a day with ginger juice and honey, or with the juices of Tulsi and *bili (bilwa)* leaves, or with *jwaraghna kwath.*

Benefits : All kinds of acute fevers, especially those mainly caused by *vata* and *kapha,* are cured by treatment with this *rasa,* which causes perspiration and brings the temperature down. If the temperature is not brought down by 3 or 4 days' treatment with this *rasa,* and typhoid is suspected, treatment with *tribhuvan keerti rasa* should be discontinued.

Kaalaari rasa : Dosage and manner of use : In case of malaria or fevers caused by the concerted action of excess of *vata* and *kapha (sannipaat jwara),* give one tablet along with Tulsi and ginger juices in an extract of 7 to 21 cloves. In an acute stage of this kind of *sannipat jwara,* administer *kaalaari rasa* with *tagaradi kwath,* or with an extract of 7 cloves, 5 grammes of fresh green *brahmi (mandookparni)* leaves, 5 grammes of *jatamansi* and 5 grammes of *shankhahuli.* In case of typhoid fever, give this *rasa* with 5 grammes of powdered nutmeg, following it up with milk, or with 2 grammes of *godanti bhasma* mixed with neem juice.

Muktāpanchāmrit rasa : Dosage : Two grammes of this *rasa* mixed with 5 grammes of the powder of the smaller variety of *peepar (piper longum)* should be given with milk collected directly from the teats of a cow that has given birth to a calf just 3 or 4 months ago.

Benefits : This medicine is beneficial in chronic fevers and tuberculosis. It is even more beneficial if administered with 8 milligrammes of *suvarna* (gold) *bhasma*.

Kumarkalyan ghrit (ghee that is beneficial for children): Dosage : 10 grammes of the *ghrit* should be administered with milk.

Benefits : Regular use of this *ghrit* imparts strength, lightens skin colour, promotes digestion, sharpens the intellect and prolongs life. Babies given this *ghrit* do not experience any discomfort or pain while cutting their teeth.

Suvarna **(gold)** *bhasma* **:** Give 5 milligrammes of the *bhasma* with 2 grammes of *sitopaladi choorna* and honey. Follow it up with warmed milk of a cow.

Benefits : *Suvarna bhasma* has a rejuvenating *(rasayan)*, invigorating *(vajikaran)*, and strengthening action; it sharpens the intellect and restores the balance of *vata, pitta* and *kapha* in the body. It is of special value in the treatment of tuberculosis, lymphadinitis, asthma, cough, anaemia, diabetes, impotence, weakness of the brain, syphilis and all disorders caused by abnormal amounts of *vata (vayu)*.

In addition to the above formulations, three other useful formulations, viz. *'adusol'*, *'kaasamrit'* and *'tulsi ark'* (essence of Tulsi) are also available almost everywhere.